JUDY MARTIN

Scraps, Blocks & Quilts

Patterns & Techniques

QUILT BLOCKS ✦ SCRAP QUILTS ✦ SAMPLER QUILTS
FRIENDSHIP QUILTS ✦ LOG CABIN QUILTS

CROSLEY-GRIFFITH
PUBLISHING COMPANY, INC.
3030 Upham Court, Denver, Colorado 80215

To Mom and Dad

Photography by Birlauf & Steen
Linotronic output by LaserWriting, Inc.
Printed by American Web

0-929589-01-7
Published by Crosley-Griffith Publishing Company, Inc.
3030 Upham Court, Denver, Colorado 80215
First Printing, 1990
15 14 13 12 11 10 9 8 7 6 5 4 3 2

TABLE OF CONTENTS

ACKNOWLEDGMENTS

Organizing the friendship quilt projects in this book provided me with a wonderful opportunity to make new friends and renew old acquaintances. It was a joy conversing or corresponding with so many generous and talented quilters. I would like to thank the following people who so kindly participated in making blocks or sending fabric and signing friendship patches for this book:

Mary Leman Austin
Jinny Beyer
Jane Blair
Georgia Bonesteel
Susan Ennis
Helen Kelley
Judy Mathieson
Marsha McCloskey
Doreen Speckmann

Catherine Anthony
Moneca Calvert
Sharyn Craig
Marianne Fons
Helen Young Frost
Harriet Hargrave
Roberta Horton
Nancy J. Martin
Mary Mashuta
Liz Porter
Vivian Ritter
Marie Shirer
Ami Simms
Helen Squire
Louise O. Townsend
Blanche Young

Faye Anderson
Barbara Brackman
Chris Wolf Edmonds
Flavin Glover
Jeffrey Gutcheon
Nancy Halpern
Bettina Havig
Carter Houck
Jean Ray Laury

Bonnie Leman
Diana Leone
Ruth McDowell
Nancy Pearson
Yvonne Porcella
Shirley Thompson

Jan Albee
Rosemary Angelos
Mary Beery
Rachel Brown
Etsuko Furusawa
Jann Hoffman
Marge Kerr
Joyce Ketterling
Janet Lyles
Emmy Midkiff
Ikuyo Saito
Shirley Wegert
Alma Wenger

Lilliams T. de Gonzalez
Marilyn Hoksbergen
Carol Huisman
Jane Hummel
Sharon K. Jolly
Margaret Karr
Dixie Loynachan
Karen Matice
Beth McMillen
Diane Myers
Linda Olivier
Min Reinertson
Wilma Rozendaal
Anne Sharkey
Karen Spencer

Cheri Spoelstra
Aileen Taylor
Elizabeth Uitermarkt
Mae Van der Wiel
Leona Vande Voort
Deanie Visser
Dorothy Vos
Carla Voss
Judy Willer

Joyce Aufderheide
Dot Bettis
Jonna Castle
Elayne Cottingham
Carol Crowley
Reni Dieball
Wendy Dodge
Betty Dufficy
Theresa Eisinger
Berniece Fair
Juanita Froese
Madelyn Gibbs
Laura Hullet
Louise Morrison
Bonnie Mulvany
Linda Nolan
Mary Coyne Penders
Libby Phillips
Angela Smith
Marla Stefanelli
Nell Torrez
Geri Waechter
Hari Walner
Margaret Waltz
Arlene Watters
Daphne Wells

Thanks also to family and friends who signed signature patches and provided advice and support, especially Steve Bennett, Marla Stefanelli, Louise O. Townsend, Janice Bennett, Mollie Bennett, Tom Bennett, Shirley Wegert, and Jill Swingle. Special thanks to Brenda Groelz for sharing her Flower Chain block.

Blocks in Judy Martin's Friendship Sampler (shown on page 112) and their makers are, from left to right: *Top row,* Mother's Day, Madelyn Gibbs; Chinatown, Dorothy Bettis; City of Angels, Laura Hullet; Kansas City, Jonna Castle; Guitar Picker, Daphne Wells. *Second Row,* San Diego Sunshine, Wendy Dodge; American Beauty, Elayne Cottingham; Girl Next Door, Nell Torrez; Baby Boomer, Theresa Eisinger; Building Block, Geri Waechter. *Third Row,* Stitcher's Square, Carol Crowley; Valley of the Sun, Arlene Watters; Vagabond, Hari Walner; Georgetown Loop, Juanita Froese; Prairie Nine-Patch, Reni Dieball. *Fourth Row,* Puppy Dog Tails, Joyce Aufderheide; Georgetown Loop, Berniece Fair; Stitcher's Square, Marla Stefanelli; Dear Old Dad, Libby Phillips; Puget Sound, Louise Morrison. *Fifth Row,* Oregon Trail, Linda Nolan; Sunday Best, Angela Smith; Smoky Mountain Block, Betty Dufficy; Judy's Star, Bonnie Mulvany; January Thaw, Margaret Waltz.

Blocks are listed alphabetically. All but a handful of blocks were designed by the author especially for this book. For the few remaining blocks, the artist is listed or the designation "trad." is used in the index to indicate a traditional pattern. (Many of the blocks designed by the author were made by others. The name of the maker is listed under the block photograph.) Following each block name in the index are page numbers for the block piecing diagram and for the blank drawing for experimentation with color. Color photographs of the blocks appear on the pages facing the corresponding block piecing diagrams.

INDEX OF BLOCK PATTERNS

INDEX OF QUILTS & QUILT PATTERNS

Quilts are listed in alphabetical order. Following the quilt name, in this order, are page numbers for the quilt photo; quilt instructions; block photo(s)--block piecing diagram(s); and blank block drawing(s) for experimentation with color.

While I was working on *Judy Martin's Ultimate Book of Quilt Block Patterns,* I found that I had too many irresistible ideas for a single book. Even before I finished that book, I began collecting material for a second volume. Over a period of two years, I shaped this material into *Scraps, Blocks & Quilts.*

Some of the features and formatting are similar to *Judy Martin's Ultimate Book of Quilt Block Patterns:* Blocks are presented with a color photo, piecing diagram, and blank block drawing for experimenting with color. Full-size patterns for blocks and sets, with seam allowances and grain arrows, are at the back of the book. Blocks are rated to indicate ease of construction. Yardage figures for each patch are included in a chart. Finally, the basic quiltmaking instructions are mostly the same in both books.

Here, the similarity ends. In *Scraps, Blocks & Quilts,* the block photos are larger. Piecing diagrams for the blocks face the corresponding photos so you can easily refer to both as you work on your project. All of the blocks are new and different; none is repeated from *Ultimate.*

The biggest difference is in the focus of this book. *Scraps, Blocks & Quilts* has plenty of block patterns, but it devotes a significant amount of space to quilts, as well. Color photos and complete patterns for twenty quilts are included. There are chapters on Scraps & Scrap Quilts, Friendship Quilts & Sampler Quilts, and Log Cabin Quilts. Other chapters take you From Blocks to Quilts and go into detail on Style in the Block.

Rather than being just more of the same, *Scraps Blocks & Quilts* complements *Ultimate* with its new slant. It makes more of a point of blocks being the basis for making quilts. Every block pattern becomes a quilt pattern, so the two-hundred patterns in this book are a real treasure trove for a quiltmaker.

Of course, the block patterns, alone, may be reason enough for you to want this book. Block collecting has been historically, and continues to be, a delightful and inexpensive hobby. Many quilters enjoy making blocks to remind them of favorite fabrics or of quilts they have made and parted with. Long ago, quilters made blocks to record patterns for future use. If you don't have time to make every quilt that comes to mind, you can make individual blocks to save your ideas for some later date. Finally, you can make blocks to exchange with friends for friendship quilts. You can exchange with people you know, or you can meet new quilters through a friendship block exchange. Either way, you will have the pleasure of sharing with other quilters, and you will produce a charming quilt full of warm memories.

Whether your interest lies in collecting blocks or in making quilts, you will find everything you need in this book. You will find clear diagrams, detailed information on style, color, scraps, techniques, and shortcuts, plus inspiring new designs for two hundred blocks and quilts. I think you will enjoy using the book as much as I have enjoyed writing it.

In this section, I present the methods that I use in quiltmaking. My approach to cutting and piecing is based on standard dressmaking procedures, and it calls for only skills and equipment that you would already possess for any other kind of sewing project. If you are a sewing enthusiast who has never before made a quilt, you will find this method natural and easy to learn. If you are an experienced quilter, you will find some helpful information in this section, as well. Even if you have your own methods, you can benefit from the suggestions for choosing fabrics, pressing, perfecting joints, and so forth.

Your choice of colors and fabrics can make a profound difference in the character of your finished block or quilt. The Saturday's Child block (page 58) that was made by Catherine Anthony looks elegant, sweet, and fresh. The same block made by Liz Porter looks intense, moody, and decidedly contemporary. Compare the block pairs on pages 54-71 to see just what a difference your choice of colors and fabrics can make.

For many of you, choosing colors and fabrics is the most enjoyable step in making a quilt. It is here that you get to exercise your creativity, to add your own personal touches to a pattern. For others of you, perhaps, choosing fabrics seems like a guessing game, one for which you haven't a clue. Of course, when you know how to play the game, you will have a lot more fun. With practice, you can get to be very good at it, too.

Since it takes so much less time to make a block than it takes to make a whole quilt, those of you who like choosing fabrics get to do it much more often as a block collector. And those who are intimidated by the prospect of choosing fabrics benefit as well. Not much time or fabric is wasted when your block is less than perfect. Often it is easy to see what you have done wrong, and better yet, you can fix it quickly and easily. Perhaps all it needs is a little more contrast here or a brighter accent there. Making blocks will give you valuable practice in choosing colors and fabrics. And with practice come skill and confidence. Once you start to have success with your color choices, you will doubtless start to enjoy this step in the quiltmaking process.

How do you get started learning the color game? What are the ground rules? Let's start with the object of the game. It is not to choose the "right" colors. It is not to choose the color combination that most people like. The object is to choose a color scheme that you like. That shouldn't be too hard, should it?

You can start by looking at the color photos of blocks in this book. Make a list of blocks whose color schemes and fabrics appeal to you. Now look at the blocks on your list again. What do they have in common? Did you choose only the blue blocks? Or the purple ones? Did you choose monochromatic blocks? Multicolored ones? Blocks with many fabrics? Or few fabrics? Blocks with soft colors? Blocks with dark, rich tones? Blocks with strong contrast? Blocks that "glow"? Blocks that have blending colors? Bright blocks? Blocks with busy prints? Blocks with prints positioned carefully for special effects? Once you start to verbalize what you like and don't like, it becomes easier to choose fabric combinations that are going to please you when you start making blocks.

If you find a block with a color scheme that you like, you can make a block just like it. Or, if you like the colors of one block and the pattern of another, you can rework the pattern in your chosen colors.

My favorite way to come up with a winning color scheme is to start with a favorite multicolored print. I then add fabrics to match the accent colors in the print. For example, I might start with a blue print with pink

COLOR & FABRIC CHOICES

roses and green leaves. I'll add prints in one or two shades of pink and a floral stripe in white with pink and green accents.

I keep a stash of fabric on hand so that when I'm gearing up to make a block or quilt, I can just start pulling fabric off my shelves. I find that buying three-quarters of a yard to one-and-one-half yards of each fabric is sufficient for most of my projects, although I may buy more if I think the fabric would make an especially nice border or alternate block. I pull down more fabrics than I need for the project at hand. In fact, I pull down anything remotely close to my intended theme. I start stacking and staggering the folded fabrics, eliminating those that detract from the mix. Sometimes, I'll hold the collected fabrics up to my stash to find a suitable accent. I try to vary the look of the prints, including prints of various sizes and characters.

Sometimes, I start with a block and then choose the colors and fabrics; at other times I start with the fabrics. Sometimes I color a block drawing, and sometimes I simply start cutting patches from fabric.

Occasionally, I'll cut a large print, floral stripe, or widely spaced motif with patches carefully centered over a particular part of the print to achieve a special effect. This adds a formal, elegant touch to a block. At other times, I'll cut patches from different parts of a large print for a casual look with an added spark of interest.

Please don't be intimidated by choosing fabrics. It is simply a matter of learning to recognize what you like when you see it. If you keep your mind open and you aren't afraid of looking foolish, you'll be in the best possible situation for learning about color. As you pull fabrics from your stash, you'll feel free to try all sorts of outlandish combinations. Some will be awful, which is pretty much what you expected, but others will be wonderfully refreshing and delightful.

Having just told you that the object of the game is to please yourself, I might appear a little foolish if I tried to establish hard-and-fast rules. You may not like the same things that I do. However, I find that verbalizing what has worked for me in the past helps me to make successful blocks time after time. Therefore, I offer for your consideration some guidelines that I follow. Feel free to adapt them to suit yourself.

1. Experiment with color combinations for your block by coloring a block drawing with felt pens, crayons, or colored pencils. If you think you'll want to try more than one coloring, photocopy the block drawing and color the copies.

2. Aim for variety in value, scale, and visual texture. That is, include light, medium, and dark shades; small, medium, and large prints; and

printed figures of many different characters: dotty, striped, fluid, regimented, organic, geometric, sparse, busy, sketchy, detailed, and so on.

3. Study your fabrics together before you start to make the block. Arrange and rearrange them to see which ones look best next to each other. Do they blend or contrast in the right places for the pattern that you have in mind? Do they appear too busy or boring together?

4. If you will be using a linear pattern, such as a stripe, is there a balanced way of using it in your pattern?

5. Cut out the block and arrange the pieces on a table or flannel board. Study the effect. Live with it for a few hours or a few days while you work on something else. A finished block always looks better than the patches on the table. Still, if you dislike the block now, you probably won't like it after you sew the patches together. Decide whether any changes would improve the block, and cut out any replacement pieces to judge their effect. By the time you are ready to sew the block, you should have ironed out any possible problems.

6. After you make the block, look at it critically. What do you especially like about it? Even if you like the block, is there something you could improve upon next time? Treat each block as a learning opportunity. You may start out learning from your mistakes, but before long, you'll be learning from your successes, as well.

I'm a self-taught quilter who made quilts for over ten years before learning how most people do it. I was astonished to find out later that people marked and cut patches one at a time. It never occurred to me to do it that way. My experience had been in dressmaking. I was accustomed to

QUICK CUTTING

pinning a paper pattern to doubled fabric when I cut. When I stitched, I guided the edge of the fabric along a seam gauge on the throat plate of the sewing machine. That's how I made my clothes, and that's how I did my patchwork, also. I probably would not be a quiltmaker today if I'd had to make that first quilt using time-consuming traditional methods. I'm not that patient. You may enjoy hand work. If so, I respect that. Please feel free to continue to make quilts your own way. However, if you've been longing for a shortcut and you are comfortable with a sewing machine, read on.

If you've ever used a sewing machine to make a simple skirt or dress, you'll find this method to be quite natural. The method is quick, accurate, and versatile, as well.

Forget about templates. Instead, you will be using paper patterns (as you do in dressmaking). The paper need not be heavy. In fact, it should be flexible. Sturdy, deluxe tracing paper or graph paper are ideal. Trace or rule your pattern with seam allowances included. (There's no need to trace the seam lines. The cutting lines will suffice.) Fold your fabric, with selvedges together, on your ironing board. Press. Fold again to make four layers, if desired. Press again. The layers should be smooth and even. Pin your pattern to the top layer, observing grain lines. (If you pin through all four layers, the pattern will bow down around the pin and flip up around the edges. It is easier to cut accurately with the pin catching only the top layer.) Cut around the pattern through all layers with good, sharp scissors.

Be careful not to shift the layers of fabric as you cut. Hold the scissors straight, not angled, so that the blades cut through all layers with a vertical stroke. If your scissors are angled, patches on the bottom layer may be larger or smaller than ones on the top layer. Use somewhat short strokes, cutting in the middle of the blades rather than at the tip or back. Cutting at the tip makes for little, mincing strokes that are jerky and inefficient. Cutting at the back of the blade lifts the fabric too much and makes it difficult to keep the layers even and the pattern in place.

Be sure to cut off the points of the patches as indicated on the patterns. This will provide clues for positioning patches for machine piecing, and it will reduce bulk in the seam allowances. Cut patches edge to edge, aligning the pattern piece with the edge already cut for the last patch. You don't need to trim off the selvedge, but avoid it when you position your pattern for cutting. The selvedge may shrink disproportionately, causing billows, or it may be printed with the manufacturer's name or have perforations or an unprinted edge that will look like a glaring error if it shows up in your quilt. It is best simply to steer clear of the selvedge.

If your pattern gets dog-eared, make a new one. Cut the largest patches first; smaller patches can be cut from the leftovers.

If you are cutting symmetrical patches, such as squares, diamonds, rectangles, isosceles triangles (having two sides the same length), kites, octagons, arrows, or trapezoids, you can turn the pattern over after you cut each stack of four. The pattern will curl up as you cut, and by turning it over, you can flatten it again.

Occasionally, a pattern calls for asymmetrical patches (ones that are different when viewed from the back). Rhombuses (G patches), parallelograms (E1-E3), and many of the more unusual triangles (such as C1-C5) are asymmetrical. If you need to cut patches and their reverses in equal numbers (that is, if you need as many C1's as C1r's), you can follow the usual layer-cutting procedure. If you need to cut asymmetrical patches without their reverses, you'll have to unfold the fabric. Cut one patch at a

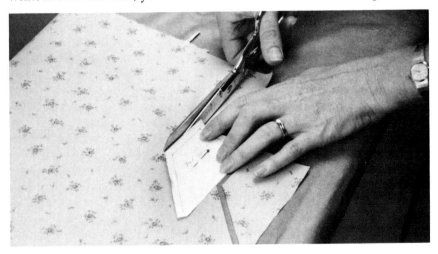

time, being careful to keep the patch right side up as you cut each patch. If you need to cut the same asymmetrical shape from several fabrics, you can layer the different materials, keeping each right side up.

That's all there is to cutting. No marking is needed. In fact, as you gain experience, you will find that you can simply hold the pattern in place with your fingers without pinning. As you cut, move your fingers as needed to keep the pattern in place. If the pattern gets jostled, simply reposition it.

PIECING PREPARATIONS

A piecing diagram is included for each block in the book to show you the piecing sequence. Still, you'll probably find it helpful to lay out your patches in their proper positions.

Pick them up as you prepare to stitch them together. I've been making patchwork quilts for more than twenty years, and I still lay out the patches for a block in this way. If I haven't done so, I'll invariably make mistakes.

In general, you will be sewing patches together to make rows or other units, which are then joined to complete the block. Go back to the patches that you have laid out on the table. Spread the patches apart between units or rows, referring to the piecing diagram.

There are three keys to precision patchwork. The first is an accurate pattern. No problem. Simply take any pattern straight from the book. The second key is accurate cutting. Simply cut your fabric patches to exactly match the patterns. The final key is accurate sewing, which boils down to following an accurate seam gauge. This is where most quilters who have problems get into trouble.

Once, I took my sewing machine to a friend's house to help her make Log Cabin drink coasters for a crafts fair. She had already cut out the strips. We set up our sewing machines at opposite ends of the kitchen table and started working. We got involved in conversation, and an hour had passed before we knew it. More conversation, more time, more little Log Cabins. At some point in the proceedings, one of us stopped working long enough to survey the growing pile of coasters. We seemed to have a problem: My blocks were a half inch larger than hers! How could that be? Different ideas of a 1/4" seam allowance, it seems. I was using a tape marker and she was using the edge of her presser foot as a guide. The difference in our seam gauges was only slight, but the difference in the completed blocks was quite noticeable. We were lucky. Log Cabin blocks are pretty forgiving, and we were able to make use of all of the coasters (in sets of two sizes), after all. We realized, though, that had we been making some other pattern, we could have had a mess on our hands. The problems arise when one part of the block has more seam allowances than another part. If your seam allowances are imprecise, then the various parts of the block will not fit together.

Check your seam gauge right now. You may be surprised to find that your seam allowances are not exactly 1/4" deep, especially if you have been using the edge of your presser foot as a guide. Here are two ways of correcting the problem:

If you like to use the edge of your presser foot as a guide, you may want to make your seam allowances match that measurement even if it is not exactly 1/4". To do this, trace or draft your pattern piece without seam allowances, leaving some space all around. Do not cut it out. Insert this pattern to the right of your sewing machine's needle with the seam line along the right edge of the presser foot and the needle outside of the patch.

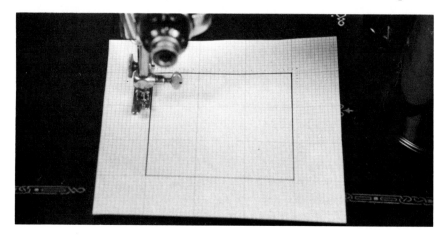

Stitch without thread, following the seam line with the edge of the presser foot. Cut along the perforations made by the needle. Be sure to do this with every pattern piece.

If you prefer exact 1/4" seam allowances, as given on the patterns in this book, you have a couple of options. If you have a zig-zag machine, you may be able to adjust your needle position to make perfect 1/4" seams using the presser foot as a guide. Simply trace a pattern from the book, including seam lines as well as cutting lines. Align the edge of the presser foot with the cutting line of the pattern. Adjust the needle until it aligns perfectly with the seam line.

If you can't adjust your needle, you can insert the pattern under the needle, lower the presser foot, and stitch on the seam line for several inches to make sure it is feeding straight. With the paper pattern still in place and the presser foot still down, put a piece of masking tape on the throat plate of the machine right along the cutting line of the pattern. Use the edge of the tape, rather than your presser foot, as a seam gauge.

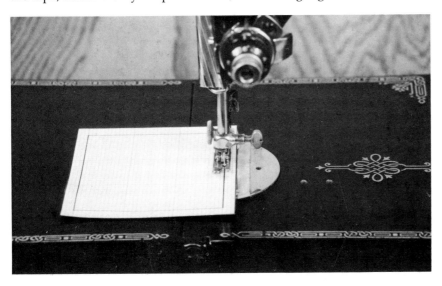

PRECISE PIECING

Years ago, when both of us were still fledgling quilters, Marsha McCloskey and I got together to share techniques and ideas. (We still do.) I showed her how I drafted paper patterns and cut them out without marking. She suggested an improvement: cutting out on the ironing board. (This was a real back saver after I'd been cutting out on the floor. Now, fifteen years later, my back and I are even more grateful to Marsha for the tip.) I introduced Marsha to a seam ripper (we all make mistakes from time to time). And I showed her how to cut off points to align the patches properly for piecing.

It was Marsha who told me about chain piecing. She described sewing one pair of patches together and then, without stopping to lift the presser foot, continuing right on stitching the next pair of patches. She said that her young daughter, Amanda, would ready the pairs of patches and hand them to her. Marsha raved about the method, but I'm afraid I resisted chain piecing for awhile because I didn't have anyone to help me get the next pair of patches ready. I'm embarrassed to say that it didn't occur to me that I could lift my foot off the pedal and pause to get the next pair of patches ready to sew myself.

Once I tried chain piecing, I was sold on it. You can sew as fast or as slowly as you like. The great advantage is that you avoid all those nasty thread ends and snarly knots that come with starting and stopping the usual way. You can save a great deal of thread (and bobbin winding), and you can avoid the tedious snipping of threads on the back of your quilt, a chore that delays your enjoyment upon completing your quilt top.

Chain Piecing Method: Join two patches in a seam, stitching from edge to edge of the patches and backtacking at both ends. Come to a stop, but leave the presser foot down. Prepare the next pair of patches. Slip the next pair of patches under the tip of the presser foot (without lifting it). Stitch through thin air for a couple of stitches until the second pair of patches reaches the needle. Stitch the second pair of patches together, backtacking at both ends. The first pair of patches will be attached by a twist of thread. Continue joining patches in pairs. Snip the threads between pairs when you are ready to go on to the next step.

Some machines balk at stitching right up to the edge of the fabric. They may push the fabric down the hole or make a huge knot on the bobbin side. This is not such a problem when you are chain piecing. With no long thread tails to tangle, the stitching proceeds more smoothly. I've found that it is also helpful to avoid stitching over the edge of the fabric in reverse. I make it a point to start and end each seam on a forward stitch. I stop about one stitch shy of the edge when I backtack, and I never have problems with snarls and tangles. For the same reason, I also make it a point to stitch from the square end of a triangle toward the pointed end wherever possible. Occasionally, the pointed end can get pushed down the hole with the needle if you start your line of stitching there.

Assembly-Line Method: Assembly-line strategies go hand-in-hand with chain piecing. With this approach, you sew all of the A patches to all of the B patches for the entire quilt. Then you add a C patch to each pair, and so on until you have completed all of the blocks. This can be tedious, and it can be dangerous. You can repeat a mistake hundreds of times before you know it. I modify the assembly-line idea to make it more interesting and to allow me to use the approach to piece a single block. Most blocks have four corners alike, so I repeat each step four times. I simply snip the chains apart as I complete the fourth repeat of each step. It is not until the final step that I have to lift the presser foot and break the chain.

For example, to make the Carnival Ride block on page 63, I start by joining a J9 patch to a C9r triangle. I repeat this step to make four of these units. I leave the last unit under the presser foot and snip apart the other three. Then I add a C14 to each of the three units. By this time, the fourth unit is clear of the presser foot, and I snip it off and attach a C14 to it. The idea is to repeat each step for the matching parts of the block without ever lifting the presser foot. The description gets a little tedious, but if you care to follow along, referring to the diagram, you can see how this works for the whole block. Next I sew a J9r patch to a C9r triangle. I repeat this step to make four such units. I leave the last unit under the presser foot, and I snip off the rest of the units. I set aside the first four units, and I add a C14 to each of the three new units. By this time, the fourth new unit is clear of the presser foot. I snip it off and add a C14 to it. Next, I snip off the other three units, and I sew each to one of the units set aside earlier to make three squares. I snip off the fourth unit and sew it to its counterpart to make a fourth square. I snip off the first two square units and join them. That frees the remaining two square units, which I snip off and join. Before stitching the final seam, I must lift the presser foot and remove the last unit.

Another way to adapt assembly-line strategies is to make two identical blocks at a time. Repeat every step for the second block, and you won't have to break the chain by lifting the presser foot at all. This works well for entire quilts, and it works well for block collectors who like to make one block to keep and a second one to exchange.

Generally, in patchwork, seam allowances are pressed to one side rather than being pressed open. This keeps the batting from seeping through the spaces between the stitches. It also forms ridges that will help you align seams perfectly at joints. Here's how:

When you are preparing to stitch across a joint, press the seam allowances in opposite directions. Hold the joint between your thumb and forefinger and slide the two halves until they stop at the ridge formed by the seam allowances. At this point, the joint matches perfectly. Stick a pin

PEERLESS POINTS & JOGLESS JOINTS

in at an angle across both sets of seam allowances, and stitch. Wherever possible, turn the unit so that you are stitching across the seam allowance on the top side before you stitch across the seam allowance on the bottom side. This prevents the unseen, bottom seam allowance from misbehaving, as it is turned the way the feed dogs force it, anyway.

Careful planning will enable you to oppose seams perfectly in many neighboring units so that the joints will fall in place quite naturally. Seam allowances remain free to be creased to either side until they are crossed by another seam. Therefore, before crossing any seam with another, think first about which way you will want to crease the allowance. Keep in mind the way that you have already pressed seams in neighboring units.

When possible, press seams the way they are inclined to go naturally. If a bulky joint forces the seam allowance away from the joint, press it that way unless there is some overriding reason to press it the other direction.

If you find that you have stitched across a seam allowance folded the wrong way, simply release the stitches for the quarter-inch or half-inch in question, turn the seam allowances properly, and restitch. Backtack and blend the new seam into the original one.

You may have noticed how some people seem to be happy with patchwork joints that miss by a quarter-inch. Others will redo a joint when it misses by one-hundredth of an inch. Different people have different standards and different purposes. One quilter may be making a quilt to enter in a contest, in which case she may be striving for perfection. Another quilter may be making quilts to keep her children warm. She may or may not be concerned about how her joints match. Each quiltmaker must seek to please herself. She must balance her enjoyment of the work with her own satisfaction with the results. If she has to redo too many joints, she may get fed up with the project. If she doesn't take the time to do an acceptable job, she may not be happy with her quilt. Fortunately, practice makes perfect, and with experience, precise joints become easier and easier to master.

PRESSING PERFECTION

In all of the quilt books that are available today, very little has been written about pressing. Still, it is an important part of every successful quilt. Sometimes, the difference between a prize-winning quilt and a loser is a simple matter of pressing.

It is important to press each fabric thoroughly before cutting patches from it. All-cotton fabrics sometimes are marbled with small wrinkles after prewashing. You won't have the opportunity to press out the wrinkles after you have cut out patches, so be sure to do that before you begin. Dampen the fabric or use steam to get out every last wrinkle. Then, after you've cut the patches, take care not to rumple the fabric too much with handling.

As you join the patches together, crease the seams to one side using your thumbnail rather than using an iron. I lay the unit on my thigh, with wrong sides out and the patch toward which I will be pressing the seam allowances on top. I then flip the top patch over so that I am looking at the right side of the unit, opened flat. I run my thumbnail along the seam line to train the seam allowance in the right direction. This is called finger-pressing. Pressing with an iron can stretch bias edges at this stage, and it should be avoided until only straight edges remain unstitched. I press my fabric before cutting patches, and I don't press with an iron again until the blocks are complete. Careful finger-pressing prevents unsightly tucks and preserves the ridges of the joints (which an iron can obliterate) to make perfectly matched joints a breeze.

Which direction is the right direction to press seam allowances? There are no hard-and-fast rules, but you'll discover some directions work better than others. Here are a few tips that my experience has taught me:

1. Generally press toward the darker fabric unless there is an overriding reason to press the other way. Usually, there isn't a problem with show-through, but pressing toward the dark won't hurt anything, and it is a good starting point that is easy to remember.

2. Be consistent about pressing each block the same way. One exception might be to press neighboring blocks opposite ways when they will be sewn side by side. That way, seams in neighboring blocks will oppose perfectly when blocks are joined.

3. Whenever possible, press away from a bulky joint so that you don't have to fold back a many-layered seam allowance, which would make it even bulkier. For example, if a seam joins two squares to a rectangle, press toward the rectangle. The seam will naturally turn this way because the single layer of the rectangle will fold more readily than the double layer of the seam allowance joining the squares.

4. For pinwheels or other situations where six or eight points come together, press all seams the same direction. That way, they'll oppose perfectly for the final seam across the joint and the bulk will be distributed as evenly as possible. Press the final seam open to further minimize the bulk.

5. When you are planning which way to press seam allowances, be sure to consider your quilting pattern. If any part of the quilting motif is closer to the seam line than 1/4", you will want to press seams away from that area so that you won't have to quilt through bulky seam allowances.

For any other rule I devised, I found so many exceptions that the rule seemed pointless. It seems best to let you learn which way to press seam allowances from observation and experience. A few blocks are shown here from the back side so that you can study which way I pressed seam allowances.

PARTIAL SEAMING

Most of the blocks in this book can be made using straight seams. For a few, you'll need to set in patches. Some blocks that cannot be made with ordinary, straight seams can be made with partial seaming if you find set-in patches intimidating.

Partial seaming is really very simple. Just stitch a straight seam from one end of the patch to an approximate halfway point. Proceed with the rest of the block in the usual fashion. Then, when the block has progressed far enough that you can complete the seam, finish stitching the partial seam.

For example, partial seaming makes easy work of the County Seat block on page 36. Join two B6 triangles as usual. Make eight units like this. Add a B6 to four of them. Sew the first such unit to the octagon with a partial seam. That is, sew halfway down the seam joining the octagon to the B6. Leave the rest of the seam free for the time being. Add the next seven units, alternating units having two B6's with units having three B6's. Start to the right of the first unit and proceed counterclockwise. Stitch with complete seams from edge to edge of the patches. Fold the first unit out of the way when you attach the eighth unit. Finally, complete the partial seam joining the first unit to the octagon and to the eighth unit.

The hardest thing about partial seaming is knowing when to do it. This book eliminates that problem by showing you exactly when to do it in the block piecing diagrams. Each partial seam is indicated by a solid line turning into a dashed line. Where this appears, at first stitch only as far as the solid line extends. Then, after you have added the unit that has the line extending out beyond the patch, you can complete the partial seam. The partial seam, when completed, extends from the far end of the line having the extension all the way up to the point where you ended the partial seam earlier.

Sometimes, a block has a number of partial seams. In each case, leave the half seam uncompleted until after the patch or unit denoted by an extended line is added.

SET-IN PATCHES

Set-in patches are nothing to fear. If you cut and stitch accurately, your set-in patches will fall into place quite naturally. The important thing to remember about set-in patches is that you must not stitch from edge to edge of the patch. You must end the stitching at the end of the seam line, leaving the seam allowance free. Remove the patches from under the needle and turn the seam allowances out of the way. Do not simply pivot the patches, leaving the needle down, and continue stitching. It doesn't really matter whether you start stitching at the set-in point or at the opposite end of the seam line. Some people, especially beginners, find it easier to start at the set-in point. That way, they can insert the needle at the proper point. If you have good control over your sewing machine, you can start at the other end and adjust the stitch to a very short stitch length as you near the end of the seam line in order to stop at the precise point desired. I usually put a pin at the end of the stitching line before I sew the seam. This tells me exactly where to stop. I pull the pin out just before it reaches the needle.

Most set-in situations involve two matching patches and one different one. I usually sew first one, then the other, of the matching patches to the different one. The final seam, then, is the one joining the two matching patches. Because these patches match, it is easier to align them perfectly for the final seam.

If you are a chain piecer, you can modify your method for set-in patches. By starting at the opposite end of the seam from the set-in, you can begin stitching without lifting the presser foot. When you reach the end of the seam line, you will have to lift the presser foot and snip threads. While you have the presser foot up, insert the next unit, starting with the set-in point. Stitch from there to the edge of the patch at the opposite end. Do not lift the presser foot. Begin the next unit without lifting the presser foot. As you can see, by alternating ends you can chain stitch half of the time.

TRICKS OF THE TRADE

Make sure your sewing machine is outfitted with a number eleven (broadcloth) needle. Anything lighter may be too fragile. Anything heavier may make unnecessarily large holes. Change the needle at the first sign of a burr. Needles are inexpensive, and a burred one can run your fabric and spoil your quilt.

Choose a neutral thread color. I usually use beige. It is not necessary to change thread to match the fabric for every seam. If you are concerned about the stitches showing, match the thread to the fabric toward which you will be pressing the seam allowances. If you have a number of bobbins wound ahead of time, some with dark thread and others with light, it is a simple matter to pop in a different bobbin when you're going to be stitching on a border or sewing a whole slew of assembly-line patches the same color. You can leave your beige thread on the top and stitch patches with a dark bobbin and the dark patch down.

Opinions vary on stitch length. I feel that 10 stitches per inch makes a perfect seam. A shorter stitch makes an unnaturally firm seam that is difficult to rip out in case of error. A longer stitch is too like gathering.

Pin long seams at intervals of about four inches. Pin at each joint to be matched, and pin borders at ends, centers, then at intervals of about four to six inches. It is not necessary to pin seams shorter than about fifteen inches when no matching is needed.

If your cutting and sewing are accurate, there should be no need to fudge. However, if you should ever need to ease one side of a seam, stitch it with the full side down. The machine will take up the slack for you.

When you place patches face to face in position for stitching, align the ends of neighboring patches. The points of the pattern pieces in this book have been pretrimmed at the proper angle to align with neighboring patches. You don't have to guess how far a point should extend, and you don't have to mark seam lines in order to align the patches properly for seaming.

Be consistent when joining patches assembly-line style. Always stitch patches with the same lead edge and the same patch on top. This way, you'll avoid careless mistakes.

To achieve an even tension when pinning a long seam, use your thumb and index finger of one hand to hold the fabric where you plan to put the pin. Use the thumb and index finger of your other hand to hold the pin. And squeeze the remaining three fingers of each hand against the heel of that hand to clamp the fabric a few inches to either side of the pin. By doing this, you can hold a six-inch length of fabric firmly and evenly.

When seam allowances cannot be opposed at a joint, pin right next to the joint on the side without the seam allowances. (That is, pin in the ditch.) Stitch right up to the pin, but remove it rather than stitching over it.

When you have stitched a seam and there is a gap at a joint, release the seam for an inch or two. Instead of putting one pin through the joint, use two pins, right next to the joint on each side. Stitch the seam again, stitching over the pins.

If after a couple of tries, a joint still slips, there are a number of remedies that you might want to try:

1. Press seam allowances opposite of the way you want them. Fold the seams back again. Now there should be more of a ridge to keep the joint aligned.

2. When you do not plan to oppose seams, oppose them for stitching, anyway. Release the seam from the point of the juncture just far enough to turn the seam allowance the right way. Restitch.

3. Try stitching from the opposite end of the seam line.

If your machine will stitch over pins without balking, use very fine, small silk pins. That way, your stitching will not waver at the pins.

Support the weight of the fabric when pinning long seams. Don't let it hang and stretch out of shape.

When the lower tension gets out of adjustment, before touching the tension knob, remove the throat plate of the machine and brush out the lint. Also brush lint from around the bobbin case area. Check the stitching again; it may no longer need adjustment.

When sewing a Scrap Quilt, sew first those patches that you think will be most difficult to pair with other fabrics. When there are just a half dozen patches left to join at any stage, pair all of the remaining patches before sewing any. This will allow you to make more attractive pairings than might be possible if you just let the piles run down to the last patch before thinking about how they will look together.

Once you have completed your quilt top and added the desired borders, you will want to give it one last, good pressing. Pick off or snip any stray threads. Now, if you haven't already planned it, it's time to think about the quilting. There are four basic kinds of quilting, as follows:

QUILTING & BINDING

1. In-the-Ditch Quilting. This quilting is directly beside the seam lines on the side without the seam allowances. In-the-ditch quilting is done "by eye," without marking. It can be a little tough to manipulate the fabric onto the needle so close to bulky seam allowances, and you will have to cross over thick seam allowances at joints. This makes it a little harder to make perfect stitches when you are quilting in the ditch, but being so close to the seam lines, the stitches tend to be barely visible, so any irregularity or unevenness is minimized.

2. Outline Quilting. This also follows the seam lines. However, it is done one-fourth-inch from the seams, just beyond the seam allowances. Since outline quilting is done around each patch, there are two lines of quilting for each seam, one on each side of it. This makes for almost twice as much quilting as there would be in the ditch. However, you won't need to cross any bulky seam allowances, and the stitching is a little faster and easier. Outline quilting shows up much better than in-the-ditch quilting, so you'll want to have small, even stitches. Outline quilting can be done "by eye" or along the edge of one-quarter-inch masking tape placed beside the seam. It is not necessary to mark the quilt before basting; simply lay down the tape (one strip at a time) after the quilt is installed in the hoop or frame. To proceed from quilting one patch to another, pass the needle into the batting for a half-inch and bring it up in the neighboring patch to start quilting there.

 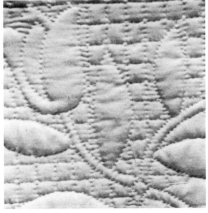

3. Marked Motifs. Alternate plain blocks, borders, sashes, and large patches are often decorated with marked motifs that run the gamut from simple to elaborate. Feathers, cables, and flowers are among the favorites. A number of suitable motifs are on pages 187-192. Marking the motifs takes some care, but quilting them is easy and the results are splendid. Mark these motifs before basting the quilt top to the batting and lining. To do this, you can position a slotted stencil over the quilt and pencil through the slots, or you can position the quilt over a black-marker drawing of the motif and trace onto the quilt top with a pencil.

4. Filler Quilting. Background patterns of interlocked circles, clamshells, grids of squares, parallel lines, or random stippling are used to fill in areas around more fanciful motifs. They serve to depress the surrounding area, making the more important motifs puff up. Straight lines can be marked with masking tape as you quilt or they can be ruled and marked with a pencil before basting. Clamshells and other designs based on circles can be marked with a pencil using an appropriate-sized cup, saucer, or jar as a template. Mark these before basting layers. Filler quilting is time-consuming, but it adds a finished look to a quilt. In times past, when cotton batting required close quilting to stay put, filler quilting was the rule. Nowadays, quilters often forgo it, since polyester batts don't need to be so firmly anchored. Still, some of the best quilts being made today boast fine filler quilting.

Before you can start quilting, you must prepare the layers. Seam together the necessary lengths of fabric to make a lining at least four inches larger all around than the top of the quilt. Press the lining, pressing seam allowances to one side. Lay the lining face down on the floor, ping-pong table, or other suitably large surface. Smooth the batting over the lining, trimming the excess batting roughly even with the lining. Center the quilt top, face up, over the batting. Baste the layers together with inch-long stitches in lines four to six inches apart. Mount the quilt in a hoop or frame. It needn't be drum-tight, but it shouldn't be entirely slack, either.

Now you are ready to begin quilting. If you have never watched an experienced quilter at work, try to arrange to do so. Many beginners are surprised when they first observe the technique. It helps to see someone doing it comfortably, especially since it may feel totally unnatural to you at first. By watching an experienced quilter you'll also have some idea of what stitch length is appropriate. The finest quilters today and in the past have managed perfect, even stitches, 15 to 20 to the inch, counting stitches on the face of the quilt only. Many quilters are satisfied with six or eight stitches to the inch. I think that most contemporary quilters aim for 10 to 15 stitches per inch now. Of course, your stitches may be longer than you'd like at first, but they will improve with time and practice. What is most important at first is using the proper technique. Without that, your quilting may never improve.

A self-taught quilter once did a small quilting project for me. It was obvious that she took pride in her work. Her stitches were perfectly even, but they were a quarter-inch long and a quarter-inch apart. I asked her to demonstrate how she quilted. She produced a long needle, which she held between her thumb and forefinger, and proceeded to stitch as if she were basting. When I showed her a few pointers and gave her a #10 betweens needle, she was able to quilt 10 stitches per inch right away. It may not be quite that easy for you, but do try the proper technique.

Cut off a 24" to 36" length of quilting thread. Thread a short needle (#8-12 betweens) with it. The thread should be a single strand with no knot. Take a stitch along the marked quilting line. Pull the thread to its halfway point, leaving a 12" or 18" tail free. Take short running stitches through all layers. The stitches should be the same length on the top and bottom surfaces of the quilt. Don't grasp the needle between your thumb and index finger; instead, push the needle from the eye end with a thimble on your middle finger. If you are right handed, use your right thumb to depress the fabric in front of the needle, and use your left thumb and middle finger below the quilt to help guide the fabric onto the needle.

This will probably feel awkward at first, especially if you are not accustomed to using a thimble. However, it is worth getting used to this method, since your fingers will get painfully sore without a thimble, and you will have difficulty achieving the desired short, even sititches unless you rock the needle from the end in this way.

When you reach the end of the thread, take a small backstitch. Then run the needle through the batting to a nearby seam line and take a small stitch right in the valley of the seam line; it will not be visible. Run the thread back in the opposite direction, along the seam line and between layers, for an inch or so. Bring the needle back out. Snip the thread directly at the surface of the quilt top and let the thread end slip back between the layers. Thread the remaining half of the first length of thread into the needle, and continue quilting.

When the quilting is completed, trim the lining and batting exactly even with the quilt top. Remove the basting stitches.

Cut a straight binding strip for each side of the quilt, with strips one and three-quarters inches wide and about two inches longer than the corresponding edge of the quilt. Press each strip in half lengthwise with right sides out.

Pin a binding strip to one edge of the quilt, with both long raw edges

of the doubled binding strip even with the raw edges of the quilt top, batting, and lining.

Trim off the excess length of the binding 1/4" beyond the raw edge of the quilt top and turn under the extra at both ends. Stitch through all layers in a 1/4" seam. Roll the binding to the back side. Pin, aligning the fold of the binding with the line of stitching just sewn.

Blindstitch by hand. Repeat for the opposite edge. For the last two edges, turn under the ends of the binding strips to be even with the binding already sewn. Stitch and roll, as before. If desired, you can turn under the excess at an angle for these last two strips to simulate a mitered corner.

Embroider your name and the date as a perfect finishing touch.

How to Use the Yardage Chart. This section includes a yardage chart to tell you how many patches you can cut from one yard of 44"-wide fabric for every pattern piece given in this book. Each pattern is listed in alphabetical/numerical order. If your quilt plan calls for more or fewer patches than the listed number, divide your number by the chart number. This will tell you how many yards are needed.

For example, if you need to cut 124 A-17 squares, find A-17 in the chart; follow that line to the right to 99, the number you can cut from one yard. Divide 124 by 99. The result is 1.25. You will need to buy about one and a quarter yards. Allow a little extra for insurance, buying an extra eighth of a yard or so.

If your quilt plan calls for fewer patches than the listed number, the procedure remains the same. For example, if you need to cut 106 A-4 squares, look up A-4 on the chart. The chart indicates you can cut 224 patches from one yard. Divide your number, 106, by the chart's number, 224. The result is 0.47, which rounds up to 0.5. You will need to buy one-half yard or a little more, perhaps five-eighths yard, for insurance.

How to Use the Quilt Dimensions Charts. This section also includes charts to tell you quilt dimensions for any block size in any set. Select the chart for your chosen set, straight or diagonal, with alternate plain squares, sashing, or adjacent blocks. Find the size of your block on the left. (For sashed sets, find the line having your block size and sash width; for pieced sashing, use the finished dimension of the complete sash unit.) Follow the line listing your block size or block size and sash width to the right to the column headed by the number of blocks per row across your quilt. (Count blocks plus alternate blocks for this.) Where row and column meet, you will find the number of inches across the finished quilt, before borders. Repeat this procedure using the number of blocks down your quilt to find the lengthwise dimension.

Here is an example. If your quilt is set straight with alternate blocks, select the first chart on page 29. Suppose your quilt plan calls for 12" blocks set in five rows of seven blocks each (18 pieced blocks alternated with 17 plain squares). Find the block size of 12" at the left. Follow that row right to the column for 5 blocks per row. Where row and column meet, you will find the crosswise dimension for your quilt, 60". Now, for the lengthwise dimension, follow the row for 12" blocks to the right to the column for 7 blocks per row. Your quilt will measure 84" in length, before borders.

TIMESAVING CHARTS

YARDAGE CHART
number of patches that can be cut from 1 yard of 44"-width fabric

SQUARES		RIGHT TRIANGLES		OTHER TRIANGLES		RECTANGLES		MISC. PATCHES		MISC. PATCHES		SASH/ ALT.BLK.	
patch	*#/yd.*	*patch*	*#/yd.*	*patch*	*#/yd.*	*patch*	*#/yd.*	*patch*	*#/yd.*	*patch*	*#/yd.*	*patch*	*#/yd.*
A1	644	B1	416	C1	384	D1	64	E1	147	G13	150	K1	12
A2	378	B2	308	C2	112	D2	112	E2	112	G14	126	K2	84
A3	357	B3	221	C3	80	D3	140	E3	90	G15	210	K3	63
A4	224	B4	285	C4	126	D4	210	E4	126	G16	147	K4	48
A5	56	B5	154	C5	210	D5	154	E5	96	G17	253	K5	42
A6	56	B6	112	C6	144	D6	231	E6	252	G18	90	K6	36
A7	154	B7	112	C7	80	D7	144	E7	264	G19	115	K7	6
A8	120	B8	144	C8	280	D8	112	E8	336	G20	96	K8	56
A9	30	B9	240	C9	176	D9	80	E9	345	G21	168	K9	42
A10	120	B10	240	C10	132	D10	273	E10	220	G22	147	K10	32
A11	80	B11	286	C11	63	D11	80	E11	198	G23	112	K11	28
A12	42	B12	180	C12	420	D12	160	E12	312	H1	126	K12	24
A13	80	B13	336	C13	120	D13	112	E13	264	H2	105	K13	4
A14	120	B14	84	C14	90	D14	126	E14	180	H3	120	K14	32
A15	180	B15	374	C15	96	D15	105	F1	200	H4	84	K15	56
A16	154	B16	500	C16	170	D16	210	F2	105	H5	147	K16	42
A17	99	B17	130	C17	322	D17	280	F3	64	H6	84	K17	24
A18	63	B18	60	C18	270	D18	392	F4	234	H7	168	K18	28
A19	63	B19	88	C19	180	D19	63	F5	105	H8	63		
A20	208	B20	192	C20	120	D20	170	F6	80	H9	144		
A21	238	B21	476	C21	140	D21	72	F7	56	H10	84		
A22	130	B22	500	C22	504			F8	90	H11	96		
A23	208	B23	437	C23	168			F9	126	H12	84		
A24	480	B24	198	C24	345			F10	196	I1	208		
A25	154	B25	70	C25	180			F11	105	I2	84		
A26	30	B26	240	C26	187			F12	126	I3	104		
A27	30	B27	70	C27	336			F13	147	I4	99		
A28	30	B28	198	C28	192			F14	63	I5	90		
A29	320	B29	540	C29	80			F15	48	I6	56		
A30	270	B30	756					F16	130	I7	168		
		B31	360					F17	288	I8	99		
		B32	144					G1	147	I9	99		
		B33	640					G2	136	I10	63		
		B34	198					G3	112	J1	154		
		B35	336					G4	175	J2	45		
		B36	390					G5	112	J3	30		
		B37	608					G6	84	J4	63		
		B38	1144					G7	70	J5	42		
		B39	1050					G8	147	J6	65		
		B40	920					G9	210	J7	168		
								G10	90	J8	30		
								G11	105	J9	55		
								G12	160	J10	20		

QUILT DIMENSIONS
SOLID OR ALTERNATE BLOCK SETS, STRAIGHT
number of inches across or down the quilt, before borders
(includes both pieced and alternate plain blocks in number of blocks per row)

Block Size	Number of Blocks per Row (across and down separately)										
	2	3	4	5	6	7	8	9	10	11	12
7″	14	21	28	35	42	49	56	63	70	77	84
7⅞″	15¾	23⅝	31½	39⅜	47¼	55⅛	63	70⅞	78¾	86⅝	94½
8″	16	24	32	40	48	56	64	72	80	88	96
8¾″	17½	26¼	35	43¾	52½	61¼	70	78¾	87½	96¼	105
9″	18	27	36	45	54	63	72	81	90	99	108
10″	20	30	40	50	60	70	80	90	100	110	120
10⅛″	20¼	30⅜	40½	50⅝	60¾	70⅞	81	91⅛	101¼	111⅜	—
11″	22	33	44	55	66	77	88	99	110	—	—
11¼″	22½	33¾	45	56¼	67½	78¾	90	101¼	112½	—	—
12″	24	36	48	60	72	84	96	108	120	—	—
12½″	25	37½	50	62½	75	87½	100	112½	—	—	—
14″	28	42	56	70	84	98	112	—	—	—	—

QUILT DIMENSIONS
SASHED SETS, STRAIGHT
number of inches across or down the quilt, before borders
(includes sashes between blocks and around the edges)

Block Size	Sash Width	Number of Blocks per Row (across and down separately)								
		2	3	4	5	6	7	8	9	10
9″	1″	21	31	41	51	61	71	81	91	101
9	1½	22½	33	43½	54	64½	75	85½	96	106½
9	2	24	35	46	57	68	79	90	101	112
9	2½	25½	37	48½	60	71½	83	94½	106	117
9	3	27	39	51	63	75	87	99	111	—
10″	1″	23	34	45	56	67	78	89	100	111
10	1½	24½	36	47½	59	70½	82	93½	105	116½
10	2	26	38	50	62	74	86	98	110	—
10	2½	27½	40	52½	65	77½	90	102½	115	—
10	3	29	42	55	68	81	94	107	120	—
12″	1″	27	40	53	66	79	92	105	118	—
12	1½	28½	42	55½	69	82½	96	109½	—	—
12	2	30	44	58	72	86	100	114	—	—
12	2½	31½	46	60½	75	89½	104	118½	—	—
12	3	33	48	63	78	93	108	—	—	—
14″	1″	31	46	61	76	91	106	—	—	—
14	1½	32½	48	63½	79	94½	110	—	—	—
14	2	34	50	66	82	98	114	—	—	—
14	2½	35½	52	68½	85	101½	118	—	—	—
14	3	37	54	71	88	105	—	—	—	—

QUILT DIMENSIONS
SOLID OR ALTERNATE BLOCK SETS, DIAGONAL
number of inches across or down the quilt, before borders
(for width, count number of blocks with a corner touching top edge;
for length, count number of blocks with a corner touching one side)

Block Size	Number of Blocks per Row (across and down separately)						
	2	3	4	5	6	7	8
10"	28¼	42½	56½	70¾	84¾	99	113¼
12"	34	51	68	84¾	101¾	118¾	—
14"	39½	59½	79¼	99	118¾	—	—

QUILT DIMENSIONS
SASHED SETS, DIAGONAL
number of inches across or down the quilt, before borders
(includes sashes between blocks and around the edges)

Block Size	Sash Width	Number of Blocks per Row (across and down separately)					
		2	3	4	5	6	7
9"	1"	28¼	42⅜	56⅝	70¾	84⅞	99
9	1½	29¾	44½	59⅜	74¼	89⅛	104
9	2	31⅛	46⅝	62¼	77¾	93⅜	108⅞
9	2½	32½	48¾	65	81⅜	97⅝	113⅞
9	3	34	50⅞	67⅞	84⅞	101⅞	118¾
10"	1"	31	46¾	62¼	77¾	93¼	109
10	1½	32½	48¾	65	81¼	97½	113¾
10	2	34	51	68	84¾	101¾	118¾
10	2½	35¼	53	70¾	88½	106	123¾
10	3	36¾	55¼	73½	92	110¼	
12"	1"	36¾	55¼	73½	92	110¼	—
12	1½	38¼	57¼	76¼	95½	114½	—
12	2	39½	59½	79¼	99	118¾	—
12	2½	41	61½	82	102½		—
12	3	42½	63¾	84¾	106		—
14"	1"	42½	63¾	84¾	106	—	—
14	1½	43¾	65¾	87¾	109½	—	—
14	2	45¼	68	90½	113¼	—	—
14	2½	46¾	70	93¼	116¾	—	—
14	3	48	72	96¼	120¼	—	—

QUILT BLOCKS IN COLOR

You will find quilt blocks not only in this chapter, but also in the Block Style, From Blocks to Quilts, Scraps & Scrap Quilts, Friendship Quilts & Sampler Quilts, and Log Cabin Quilts chapters. Similar blocks are grouped together so that you may better observe their differences. For easy reference, block photos and the corresponding block piecing diagrams are on facing pages. In a separate chapter beginning on page 130, you will find a coloring book of the blocks. The blocks appear in the same sequence here as they do in the diagrams. The caption below each diagram indicates a page number for the coloring book block.

I designed block variations related to many of the blocks in the photographs. Because of their similarity to the photographed blocks, I did not feel it was necessary to make these and show them in color. However, I thought you might enjoy having the additional patterns. Often, you may want to change the details of a block to suit your fabrics. Perhaps, you want to divide a center square into four triangles to take advantage of a striped fabric. You won't have to draft the new patterns if you find what you are looking for in one of these bonus blocks. These blocks give you many ideas for changing the details. With the piecing diagrams, coloring book blocks, and pattern pieces included for these variations, you can find just the details you are looking for, and easily plan your own colors and make the block. The photographed blocks will provide color ideas that you can use for the bonus blocks, as well. If you are feeling quite adventurous, you can design your own original blocks by mixing and matching block centers, corners, and so on, from related blocks.

In the caption below each diagram is the block name followed by the block size, the pattern rating and the page number for the coloring book drawing. As well, a helpful hint is provided for each block.

HOW TO USE THE PATTERN RATINGS

Patterns are rated for ease of construction, using a scale from A (easiest) to E (most difficult). None of the patterns in this book is particulary difficult, though some might prove a little frustrating for a beginner. Consider patterns rated "C" to be average. An "A" rating was given to the simplest of blocks, those made entirely from squares and rectangles. A "B" rating indicates a very easy block having some right triangles. A "C" block is a typical block. It may have a variety of shapes to assemble in a number of units, but the construction is generally straightforward. A "D" block has more joints to match, more bias edges, or partial seaming. The E blocks have set-in patches. If you are comfortable setting in patches, then you will find any block in this book quite makeable, regardless of the pattern rating. Many of the "C," "D," and "E" blocks would be considered quick and easy by an experienced quilter. Some of the "D" and "E" blocks may require your concentration. Although they are not exceptionally difficult, the "D" and "E" blocks might be a challenge for beginners until they have gained some confidence in their patchwork skills.

Pattern ratings also include a numerical designation. This indicates the number of patches per square foot that the pattern involves. For 12" blocks, the number is the same as the number of patches in the block. For other block sizes, the number of patches is adjusted by the proper factor to account for the size difference. The assigned numbers, then, can be readily compared. Numbers for the blocks in this book range from 15 to 91; 42 patches per square foot is the average for the blocks in this book. Seventy percent of the blocks here have fewer than 50 patches per square foot. The higher the number, the more time and patience will be required to make the quilt.

HOW TO READ THE DIAGRAMS

Letters in the diagrams refer to the full-size pattern pieces on pages 154-192. The drawings show not only the patch letters, but also the piecing sequence. The first patches to be sewn together are shown already joined into rows or other units. These units are then joined to make larger units until the last units are joined to complete the block. The diagrams often show units completely exploded in one corner, with each progressive corner having the units joined one step further.

A dashed line in the diagram is used to indicate a partial seam. The dashed end of the seam should be left free until after the unit indicated by an extended line is added. Then the partial seam can be completed.

A dot in the diagram indicates a joint where a patch must be set in. At the point marked by the dot, stitch only to the end of the seam lines rather than stitching all the way to the cut edges of the patches. This will leave the seam allowances free to pivot as needed.

A pattern letter followed by an "r" indicates that the patch is the reverse of the pattern given in the book. Turn the pattern face down on the fabric to cut reverses.

CREDITS

The majority of blocks in this book were designed and made by Judy Martin. There are a few traditional blocks, and these are marked "trad." under the block photograph. The Flower Chain block was designed by Brenda Groelz and made by the author. In order to show a variety of block styles, many of the blocks designed by Judy Martin were made by others. For these blocks, the maker is listed under the block photograph.

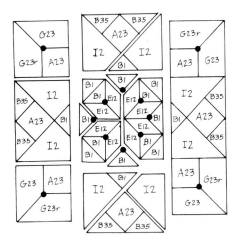

A Connecticut Yankee, E41, 14", pg. 130

This block has 12 set-in patches, but it is well worth the effort. A border stripe frames the block nicely.

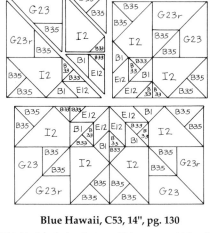

Blue Hawaii, C53, 14", pg. 130

This block looks intricate, and it has many patches, but the sewing is simple, with no set-in patches.

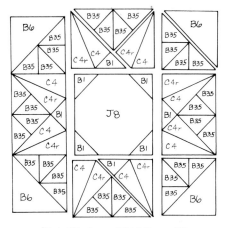

Chantilly Lace, C45, 14", pg. 130

There are lots of patches here, but the sewing is easier than it looks.

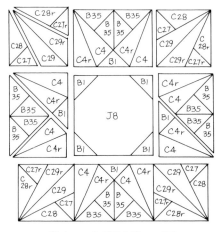

Potpourri, C48, 14", pg. 130

Take care to stitch the longest edge of the C27 patch to the C24 patch. Don't stretch the bias edges.

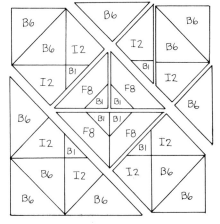

Magic Moment, C24, 14", pg. 130

This easy block is enhanced by the use of border striped fabric, cut for special effect.

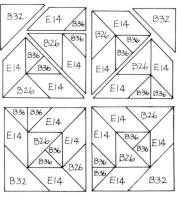

Lake of the Woods, C44, 12", pg. 130

Each of the center diamonds is cut from exactly the same part of the print for a kaleidoscopic effect.

A Connecticut Yankee, Mary Beery

Blue Hawaii

Chantilly Lace, Rachel Brown

Potpourri, Mary Beery

Magic Moment

Lake of the Woods

Spinning Wheel, Linda Olivier

Scarborough Fair, Jann Hoffman

Square Dance, Wilma Rozendaal

Pygmalion, Janet Lyles

Cape Cod Block, Marge Kerr

A Summer Song, Rosemary Angelos

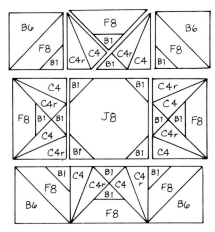

Spinning Wheel, C33, 14", pg. 130

The central octagon is a good place to show off a lovely quilting motif or a pretty decorator print.

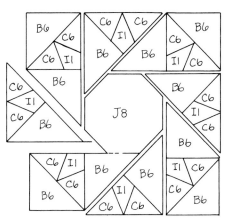

Scarborough Fair, D27, 14", pg. 130

This block goes together easily if you stitch the first unit to the octagon with a partial seam.

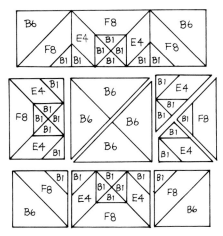

Square Dance, C38, 14", pg. 130

There is actually a star hidden within this block. An interesting use of prints gives this block pizzazz.

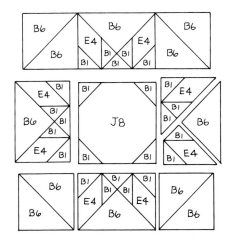

Pygmalion, C33, 14", pg. 130

This block can look traditional or contemporary, depending on your choice of fabrics.

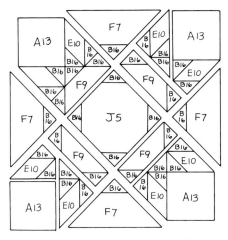

Cape Cod Block, C42, 14", pg. 130

This block is pretty set with plain sashes. Quilt parallel lines in the background to make the star stand out.

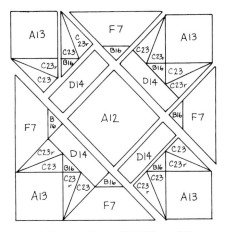

A Summer Song, C27, 14", pg. 130

For a completely different effect, cut the C24 patches from two shades of the same color.

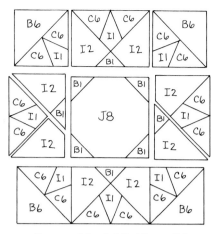

Treasure Island, C33, 14", pg. 131

This block is similar to Scarborough Fair, but it is made without partial seaming.

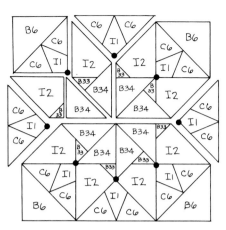

Great Expectations, E38, 14", pg. 131

This block can be made with partial seams, but the patches are small, so setting in may be easier.

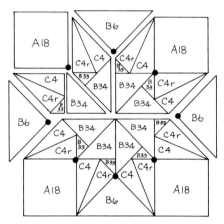

Riverboat Block, E29, 14", pg. 131

This block is not especially difficult, but it does involve set-in patches.

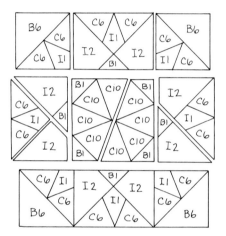

The Wild Wood, C38, 14", pg. 131

This block is similar to Treasure Island, but this center has possibilities for kaleidoscopic effects with prints.

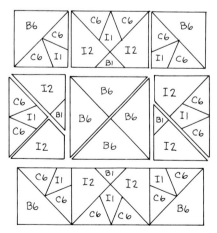

North Woods, C32, 14", pg. 131

Here is another variation of Treasure Island, with the block center divided differently.

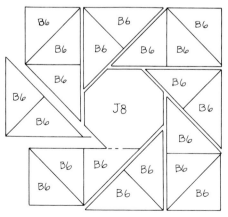

County Seat, D15, 14", pg. 131

This block is quite simple, though it has a partial seam. The large patches are perfect for fancy quilting.

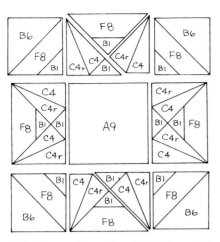

Chattanooga Choo Choo, C30, 14", pg. 131

This block is similar to the Spinning Wheel. Combine several related blocks such as this in a single quilt.

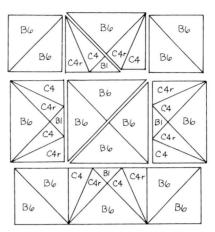

Chesapeake, C26, 14", pg. 131

The four triangles forming the central square can be cut from the same part of the print for a special effect.

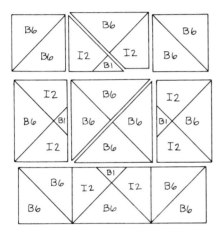

Cotton Candy, C21, 14", pg. 131

This is the easiest of the star variations. Set the blocks with plain sashing for a traditional-looking quilt.

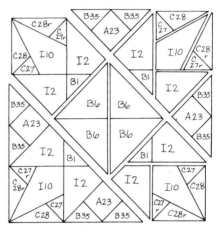

Hope & Glory, C35, 14", pg. 131

This is a variation of Saturday's Child (pg. 58). The center is divided into triangles for special fabric effects.

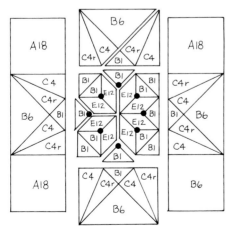

Sports Fan, E35, 14", pg. 131

This is an exceptionally pretty block, well-suited to scraps. The central star has eight set-in patches.

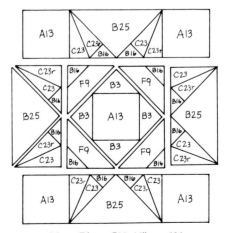

Moon River, C33, 14", pg. 131

This block would be pretty in a theme-and-variations quilt with Cape Cod Block and A Summer Song.

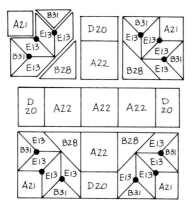

Old-Timer's Favorite, E41, 12", pg. 131

This block has an antique look. It is exceptionally pretty scraps. Be aware that it has set-in patches.

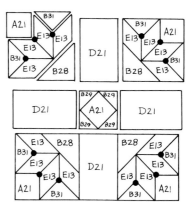

God's Green Earth, E41, 12", pg. 131

This block would be striking in an old-fashioned red, green, gold, and white color scheme. It has set-ins.

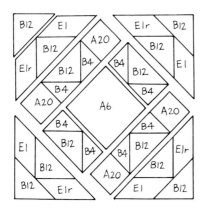

Village Green, C33, 12", pg. 131

This would make a pretty quilt in multicolored scraps. Press seams toward the center square for crisp points.

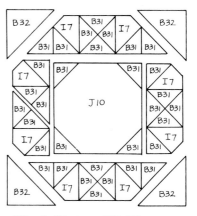

Wheel of Fortune, C45, 12", pg. 132

This block is great in light and dark blue and white with triple sashing and Nine-Patch setting squares.

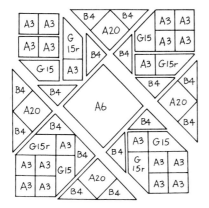

Blue Bayou, C49, 12", pg. 132

This block forms an interesting secondary pattern when set with Four- or Nine-Patch setting squares.

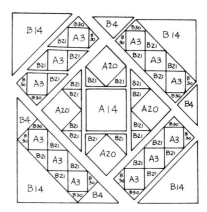

Purple Mountain Majesties, D69, 12", pg. 132

This block has simple shapes, but there are many points and joints to match. Observe the grain arrows.

Old-Timer's Favorite

God's Green Earth

Village Green, Aileen Taylor

Wheel of Fortune, trad.

Blue Bayou

Purple Mountain Majesties, Joyce Ketterling

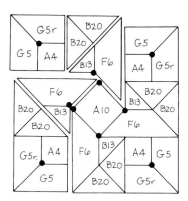

Rhapsody in Blue, E29, 12", pg. 132

This block can be made with four set-ins and four partial seams or with eight set-ins.

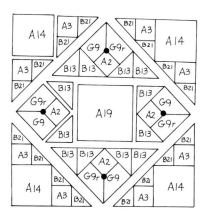

Strawberry Fields, C53, 12", pg. 132

Cut the small squares from the same fabric as the adjacent large squares for a stair-stepped effect.

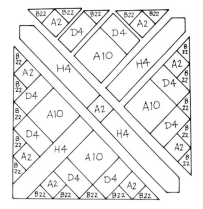

American Abroad, C45, 12", pg. 132

For an especially handsome two-block quilt, set American Abroad alternately with A Summer Place.

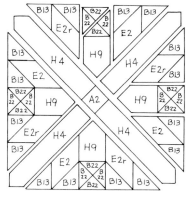

Wednesday's Child, C49, 12", pg. 132

You can cut the asymmetrical E patches from folded fabric for the required mirror images.

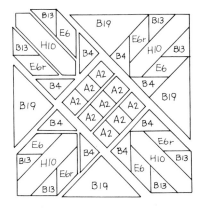

A Summer Place, C41, 12", pg. 132

E6 patches are not true diamonds; cut mirror images and always join the straight-grain edge to B13.

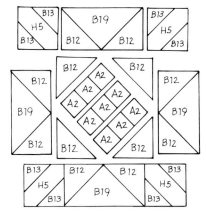

Shropshire Lad, C37, 12", pg. 132

This Mexican Star variation looks good set with blocks side by side. For something different, use scraps.

Rhapsody in Blue

Strawberry Fields

American Abroad, Cheri Spoelstra

Wednesday's Child

A Summer Place

Shropshire Lad, Diane Myers

The Land of Nod, Aileen Taylor

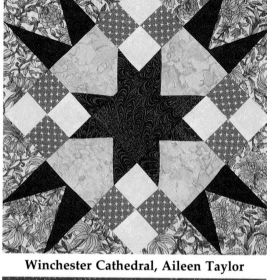

Winchester Cathedral, Aileen Taylor

Pins & Needles, Linda Olivier

Heaven & Earth, Lilliams T. de Gonzalez

Sunday's Child

Camelot, Joyce Ketterling

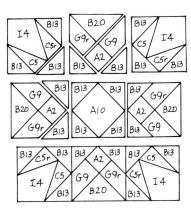

The Land of Nod, C53, 12", pg. 132

Depending on how you color it, as many as three different stars can appear in this block.

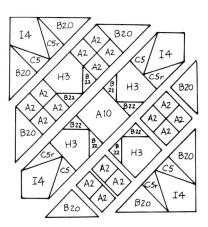

Winchester Cathedral, C49, 12", pg. 132

This is appealing in a variety of scraps, with the central stars always cut from the same solid color.

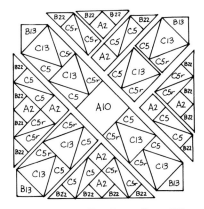

Pins & Needles, D69, 12", pg. 132

Combine this with the next three blocks plus A Stitch in Time and Alice's Adventures for a super sampler.

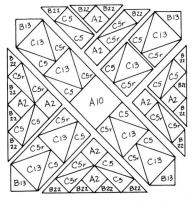

Heaven & Earth, D69, 12", pg. 132

Be sure to cut off the points of the patches according to the pattern. This will help you align patches perfectly.

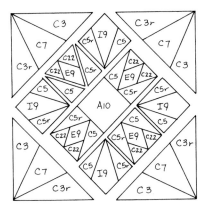

Sunday's Child, C45, 12", pg. 132

For another variation, turn the square units with the I patches so the narrow points are on the block's edge.

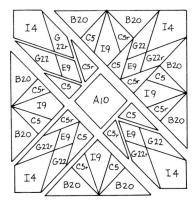

Camelot, C45, 12", pg. 132

This block makes a stunning quilt when set with sashes or alternate plain blocks.

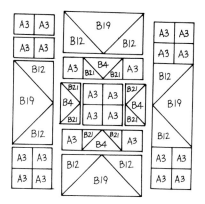

Country Comforts, B48, 12", pg. 133

This block forms a secondary pattern of chains when set with K9 sashes and A3 setting squares.

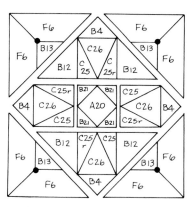

Wabash Cannonball, E37, 12", pg. 133

This block is handsome with striped fabric for the F patches. Or make F's in two shades for a chiseled look.

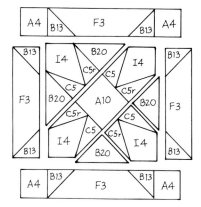

Home on the Range, C33, 12", pg. 133

This simple block looks wonderful in scraps. Vary the background fabric, as well, for extra punch.

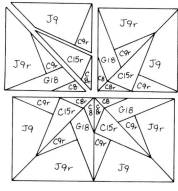

Silent Night, C32, 12", pg. 133

Combine this block with Moonlight Serenade, Carnival Ride, and Peace on Earth for a Sampler Quilt.

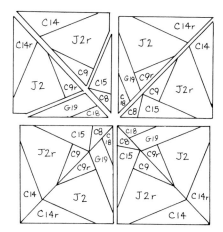

Amazing Grace, C29, 14", pg. 133

This block forms a lovely secondary pattern of stars when set side by side. Color the corners in two shades.

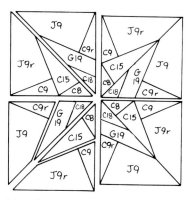

Moonlight Serenade, C32, 12", pg. 133

Cut the J patches from a striped fabric to make a handsome frame for this block.

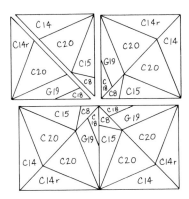

Joy to the World, D32, 12", pg. 133

Set this block with 1" sashes. You'll avoid twelve points converging, but you'll still see the star corners.

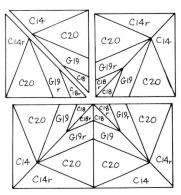

Daydream, C32, 12", pg. 133

Set blocks side by side, with the C14 patches a shade darker than C14r. A stripe would be good in C19.

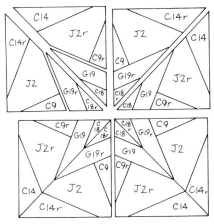

Torchlight, C29, 14", pg. 133

Set these blocks alternately with Amazing Grace or Friday's Child for a wonderful two-block quilt.

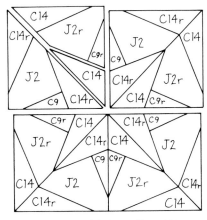

Friday's Child, C24, 14", pg. 133

Cut C's in two shades of each of three colors, with the reverses darker than the corresponding patches.

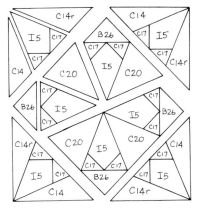

King of the Road, C40, 12", pg. 133

Press seam allowances all the same direction to oppose for the final seam. Press the final seam open.

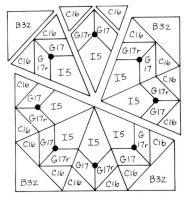

Butcher's Block, E44, 12", pg. 133

To avoid set-in patches, you can substitute two C17's and a B26 for each G17-G17r pair.

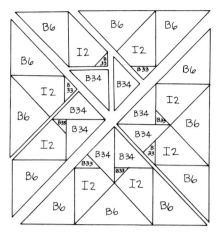

Delft Star, C26, 14", pg. 133

This block is fabulous with stripes in the background. Set blocks side by side or with sashes.

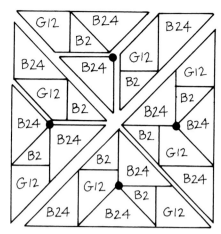

America, the Beautiful, E41, 10", pg. 133

This block has set-in patches. Stitch only to the end of the seam line at the points marked by dots.

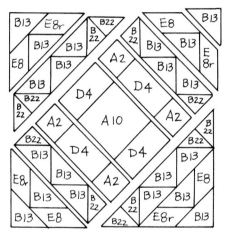

April Love, C71, 10", pg. 133

This block is delightful made from scrap fabrics. Set with plain sashes for relief from the busyness.

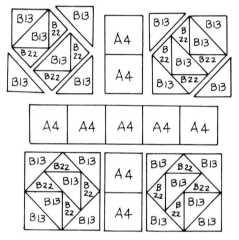

Wilderness Trail, C71, 10", pg. 134

Try this block set with one of the pieced sashes on page 81. Wilderness Trail is a natural for scraps.

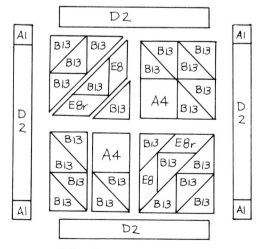

Calico Country, C55, 10", pg. 134

Cut the D patches from scraps, and set blocks side by side. Turn blocks differently for a jaunty look.

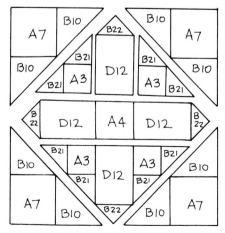

Heart of Gold, C48, 10", pg. 134

Set Heart of Gold blocks with K4 sashes and A4 setting squares. Stripes are effective in the D patches.

Delft Star

America, the Beautiful, Linda Olivier

April Love, Jan Albee

Wilderness Trail

Calico Country

Heart of Gold

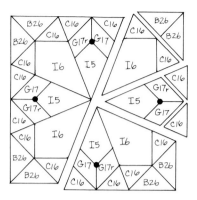

The Wild West, E40, 12", pg. 134

*Careful use of striped fabric in the background tri-
angles and the G patches makes this block sing.*

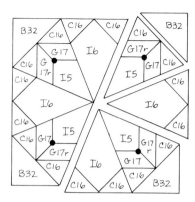

Thursday's Child, E36, 12", pg. 134

*Press all seam allowances clockwise to oppose perfectly
at the center. Press the final seam open.*

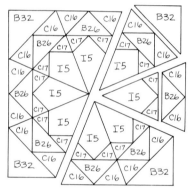

Summertime Blues, C52, 12", pg. 134

*This block would also be pretty in a counterchange of
two fabrics, with each light patch surrounded by dark.*

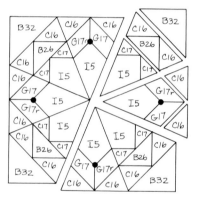

Field of Dreams, E48, 12", pg. 134

*Stitch only to the end of the seam line when setting the
I patch into the angle formed by the G patches.*

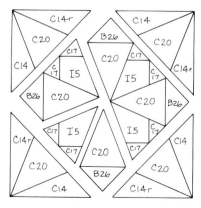

Black Beauty, C32, 12", pg. 134

*Set blocks with alternate plain squares to match the
C14 patches for a secondary pattern of circles.*

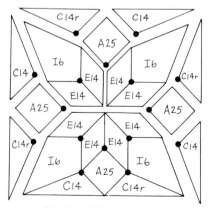

Stardust, E24, 12", pg. 134

*Because of its old-fashioned look and its many set-in
patches, this block is a good candidate for hand piecing.*

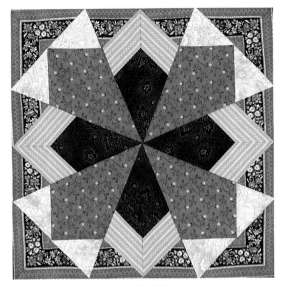

The Wild West

Thursday's Child

Summertime Blues

Field of Dreams

Black Beauty, Emmy Midkiff

Stardust

Banker's Hours, Emmy Midkiff

Charleston Quilt

Clothes Line, Alma Wenger

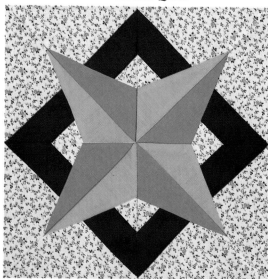

Thunder Bay, Lilliams T. de Gonzalez

Dutch Tulips, Wilma Rozendaal

Businessman's Special, Jann Hoffman

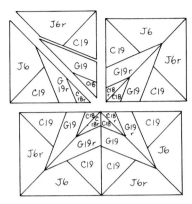

Banker's Hours, C32, 12", pg. 134

This block was designed with stripes in mind. Any of the patches can be enhanced with careful use of stripes.

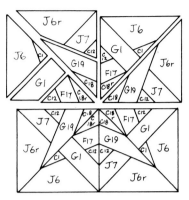

Charleston Quilt, C44, 12", pg. 134

This is my favorite pattern in the book. The interwoven effect is achieved with all straight seams.

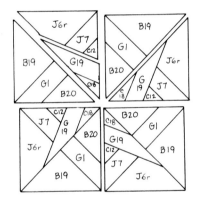

Clothes Line, C32, 12", pg. 134

This block would make a lively quilt in multicolored scraps. Set blocks side by side or with sashes.

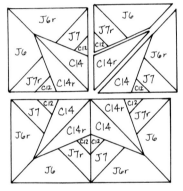

Thunder Bay, C32, 12", pg. 134

This block also looks special with J patches cut carefully from striped fabric.

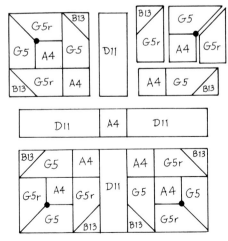

Dutch Tulips, E27, 14", pg. 134

Set blocks side by side or with 2" sashes. Use a variety of scraps in flower colors.

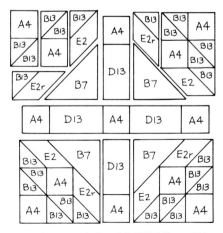

Businessman's Special, C39, 14", pg. 134

Here's a handsome block for the man in your life. Pieced sashing would be very effective here.

STYLE IN THE BLOCK

Each quilter, as she creates a quilt, makes certain decisions that affect the way the quilt looks. She makes choices all along the way. Choosing a block is just the beginning. Next, there is a color scheme; then, the decision whether or not to use scraps. Selecting a fabric palette and determining where to place each fabric in the block or quilt are two decision-making areas that define your style.

Undoubtedly, some of these style decisions are very quickly made. Certainly, they are nothing to fret over. Most quilters enjoy this part of the quiltmaking process. Other quilters keep the decision-making to a minimum by following a pattern. Even following a pattern involves decisions: Shall I follow the pattern exactly or make this or that change? Or: I can't find any fabric like the one shown, what shall I substitute? There is simply no avoiding some decisions, and it is these decisions that make each quilt unique.

No two people will make all of the same choices, and so each quilter imbues her quilt with her own distinct style. If 20 quilters each made a quilt from the same block pattern, 20 very different quilts would result. (Seeing these differences is the fun of the quilt challenge projects that are so popular today. Each participant makes a quilt incorporating specific fabrics or pattern elements, and when the quilts are done, everybody enjoys a show-and-tell session.)

Style is basically a reflection of personal taste. Every quilt has style, whether you spend much or little time making the decisions. Some style decisions are made over a period of time. Your stash of fabrics isn't created in an instant, for example. And every time you use a fabric from your stash, decisions made long ago (or recently) come into play. We all gravitate toward the things we like. This makes easy work of all the decision-making. We just do what we do because that's the way we like it. We may not even be aware that we are making some of the style decisions that define our quilts.

Sometimes, verbalizing these things and making a conscious point of thinking about style elements can help us work through something that doesn't quite satisfy us. It can also help us out of a style rut when we're ready to move on.

Here are some style decisions that you might want to think about. Select some photos of blocks and quilts that you like, and ask yourself the following questions to get some idea of style factors that you find pleasing.

QUESTIONS OF STYLE

COLOR

Shall I use a color scheme?
What kind of colors--bright? grayed? pastel? dark?
How many colors? How many shades of each?
How much variance within a color?
How much contrast between colors?
How much matching? clashing or color tension?
Which colors shall I use?
Where shall I place each color?
Shall I place colors in a conventionally balanced arrangement? asymmetrically?
Shall I place colors the same way in each block?

FABRIC

What types of fabrics shall I use? calicoes? plaids or stripes? large prints? border stripes? tone-on-tone prints? solids? textures?
How many fabrics? just a few? dozens of scraps? hundreds of scraps?
What prints shall I put together in any given pair of patches? (This is a decision usually made quickly while sewing.)
Shall I cut patches from any special part of the print?
Shall I use the fabric grain in a special way?

These elements can be mixed and matched to make a block or quilt in your own style. Style is a matter of personal taste. One likes simplicity; another likes movement. Basically, it comes down to how busy you like your quilts. There is a point for each person where she will say a quilt is too busy and another point at which she will say a quilt is too repetitive. Between these two extremes is her individual comfort zone, with the perfect balance *for her* of busyness and repetition. Some design elements add to the busyness; some offer relief from it. Consider including items from the two lists below to find your own personal balance.

THE MORE-BUSY, LESS-BUSY CONTINUUM

MORE BUSY	LESS BUSY
high contrast	blending, low contrast
strong colors	grayed, soft colors
fabrics that read as prints from a distance	solids or prints that read as solids
multicolored prints	tone-on-tone prints
many different colors	few colors
many different fabrics	few fabrics
broad range within a color	each color narrowly defined
complex block	simple block
lively set	simple set
many shapes	similar shapes
little repetition	much repetition
shifts in the value pattern	uniform value
secondary patterns emerge where blocks meet	distinct blocks

Too much busyness is overwhelming. Too much repetition is boring. When a quilt makes you squirm for either of these reasons, you will know the problem at a glance. Of course, a quilt sometimes doesn't make you squirm, it just leaves you feeling a little dissatisfied. The repetition/busyness factor may be just a little bit outside your comfort zone. Study a variety of quilts at your next quilt show, or just look at quilt photos in books to get a good idea of what your own personal comfort zone is.

CELEBRITY STYLE

Each quilter's work reflects a different style, depending on her approach to design, color, and fabric combinations. I asked a number of well-known quilters to share with you their way of working. Here and on pages 60-61 are their responses. Many of them made blocks, which you can see on pages 55-58.

FAMOUS QUILTERS TALK ABOUT STYLE

Catherine Anthony is the author of *Sampler Supreme* and co-author of four pattern books. She selects fabrics before she chooses a block pattern. She "auditions" patches on a design wall, frequently making changes as the quilt progresses. Her quilts include just about every type of fabric except small calicoes and unusually textured fabrics. Catherine says, "I mix and match everything--styles, colors, fabric, techniques, ideas, sizes, etc.... Mostly I go with the whim of the moment. Thank goodness we don't have to choose just one way of doing things."

Jinny Beyer is the author of five quilting books, including *Patchwork Patterns*, and *The Quilter's Album of Blocks and Borders*. She also designs a line of cotton print fabrics. Jinny's distinctive style reflects a strong oriental influence. She never uses solids, preferring prints that read as solids. Jinny always includes border prints in her quilts. She does all of her designing in black and white. After establishing values, she selects a color palette to correspond to the shades in her black and white sketch. Most of her quilts have at least 50 different fabrics.

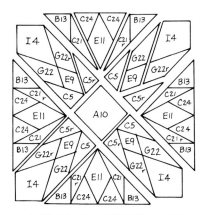

A Stitch in Time, D53, 12", pg. 135

This block has no set-ins or partial seams, but the narrow points will require accuracy and patience.

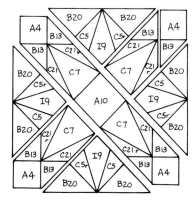

Sea of Tranquillity, D45, 12", pg. 135

This block is made with all straight seams. The many narrow points may be difficult for beginners.

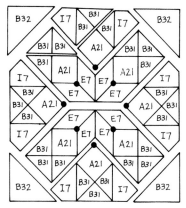

Boston's Best, E52, 12", pg. 135

This block, with eight set-ins, is not easy to make, although an experienced quilter need not hesitate.

Sharyn Craig's block, at the right, is made from several fabrics in rich, deep colors. A large, almost tropical-looking floral provides the basis for the color scheme. This one multicolored print plays off several tone-on-tone prints of different scales and visual textures. The bright white background provides a stark contrast to the other prints. Marie Shirer's block, at the far right, also includes a large, multicolored print and several tone-on-tone prints. The prints look less like solids in Marie's block. The colors are bright and clear. Whereas Sharon's block has the moody feel of a jungle, Marie's has the airy feel of a flower garden. Marie's block has stronger contrast between the star points, but the background blends into the star more here than in Sharon's block.

Mary Mashuta's block is essentially monochromatic, subtle and decidedly contemporary. It has gradually shifting colors in pastel and neutral solids. A mottled background fabric and two striped fabrics of blended pastels and neutrals complete the mix. The slight shifts in color and the asymmetry of the color placement provide the interest. Vivian Ritter's block is also monochromatic. The value contrasts are more of a point of interest here, with areas of blending and strong contrast. The printed motifs layer the block with an interesting visual texture. Prints range from tiny to fairly large; some are predictably rhythmic, while others are irregularly spaced. All of the prints are finely detailed, to add interest upon close inspection.

Marsha McCloskey's block is dark and bright, with light introduced only sparingly in areas within the darker prints. The colors are nearly complements, augmented with neutral brown. Prints range from very large to tiny; several are multicolored. Two or more shades of each color give the block depth. Susan Ennis' block is made in similar colors, although the tones are softer. A stunning large floral is centered in the diamonds, squares, and triangles for a voluptuous, graceful effect. Patches run together, with the overall kaleidoscopic design more important than the individual patch shapes. An unusual striped fabric, also cut with special care, provides the light accent that encircles the star. Prints vary in scale, but all are finely detailed.

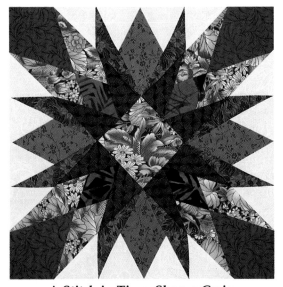

A Stitch in Time, Sharyn Craig

A Stitch in Time, Marie Shirer

Sea of Tranquillity, Mary Mashuta

Sea of Tranquillity, Vivian Ritter

Boston's Best, Marsha McCloskey

Boston's Best, Susan Ennis

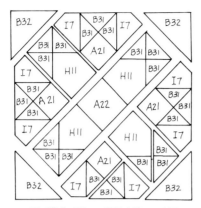

Twilight Time, C45, 12", pg. 135

Pay more attention to the lines than the grain when cutting plaid patches. Be careful not to stretch biases.

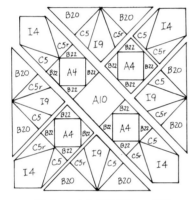

Sir Lancelot, C53, 12", pg. 135

A theme-and-variations sampler of blocks with changes in value placement would be a natural.

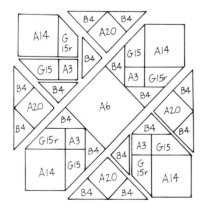

Wonderful World, 12", C37, pg. 135

Cut the G patches in mirror images by folding the fabric and cutting through two or four layers at a time.

Roberta Horton's block, at the right, is made principally from plaids. The corner triangles are solids in four slightly different tones. A marbled print adds a pleasing curve to complement the linear effect of the plaids. Contrasts are strong, with nuances of color and visual texture adding depth to the design. Ami Simms' block, at the far right, is made from hand-dyed fabrics with a mottled appearance. The unevenness of the colors adds subtlety and interest to the block. The uniformity of value is interrupted by black accents, which provide the contrast necessary to develop the pattern. Ami's block and Roberta's block differ in color placement and value placement, as well as in the nature of the fabrics.

Harriet Hargrave's block, at the right, includes prints in a variety of visual textures. The contrast of colors is sharp, with well-defined points in the outer star, and some blending in the inner star. The fabrics are similar to ones that you might find in an antique quilt, yet they look contemporary, as well. Helen Young Frost's block, at the far right, mixes brilliant colors with black accents and a beige background. Prints that read as solids are placed between multicolored patches to provide a distinct edge for each patch. Small dots and medium and large florals in an interesting montage of Country French, Oriental, and American Country motifs give this block an eclectic, almost exotic look.

Nancy Martin's block, at the right, includes small, medium, and large prints in a sophisticated, grayed color scheme. Patches are cut from the large print not quite randomly, but casually. The boldest part of the print was incorporated into the center square, but the background patches were cut from the plainer parts of the print. The G patches are cut from a carefully centered stripe. Moneca Calvert's block, at the far right, features clear bright colors and unique prints. The center square, with its large, busy print, blends into the neighboring star points. These two fabrics have similar colors and equally lively prints. The remaining prints are subtle and delineate the patches cleanly.

Twilight Time, Roberta Horton

Twilight Time, Ami Simms

Sir Lancelot, Harriet Hargrave

Sir Lancelot, Helen Young Frost

Wonderful World, Nancy Martin

Wonderful World, Moneca Calvert

Piecemaker's Block, Helen Squire

Piecemaker's Block, Blanche Young

Baker Street Puzzle, Louise O. Townsend

Baker Street Puzzle, Marianne Fons

Saturday's Child, Liz Porter

Saturday's Child, Catherine Anthony

Helen Squire's block, at the far left, is made from two mid-sized floral prints, two solids, and a floral stripe. The prints and stripes are cut carefully to center the print in the patch. The patch edges between the squares are obscured because of matching colors. Elsewhere, the contrasts define the shapes crisply. Colors are soft and contrasts are moderate, for a delicate look. In Blanche Young's block, at the left, contrasts are also moderate. The light background fabric is almost a medium. Medium-dark, medium, and medium-light gray squares blend together to provide an interesting surface over which the star appears to be laid. Many of the fabrics are tone-on-tone prints, and they overlay the block with fine detail. Two more versions of this block are on page 70.

Louise O. Townsend's block, at the far left, includes bright colors as well as medium darks and medium lights. The patches are well defined, with clean edges. The prints vary in scale, with small calicoes, mid-sized florals, a radiant stripe, and a large paisley. The color scheme is unusual and dynamic. Two shades of each color give the block depth. Marianne Fons' block, at the left, is monochromatic with black accents. The prints are clean-edged and geometric. The combination is unusual in that it has no mottling, blending, or finely textured detail. The effect is two-dimensional, which provides an interesting contradiction to the interwoven block. The solid background provides good definition for the patch shapes.

Liz Porter's block, at the far left, is intensely bright and dark. Shapes are obscured by a large, busy print. Patches are cut from different parts of this print to lend variability to the coloring. Green and magenta accents blend with the print in some places and contrast in other places. A solid black background intensifies the colors in this exotic block. Catherine Anthony's block, at the left, looks entirely different in its serenity. Colors are fresh and gentle overall, but contrasts are distinct. A large floral motif is centered in the patches. A lightly spattered print adds relief. It also adds a glowing quality because of its variegated tones. A delicately striped background frames the block. Each fabric is unusual and interesting upon close inspection, without calling attention to itself in the overall design.

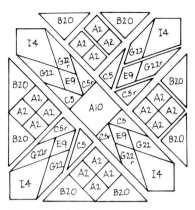

Piecemaker's Block, C49, 12", pg. 135

This block makes a beautiful Scrap Quilt. Use a different set of fabrics for each block. Set with sashes.

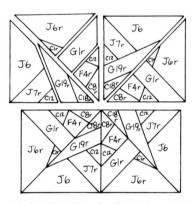

Baker Street Puzzle, C44, 12", pg. 135

Press seam allowances in opposite directions in neighboring units to help you align joints perfectly.

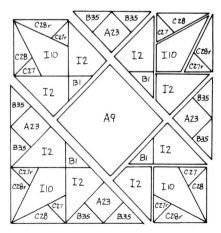

Saturday's Child, C33, 14", pg. 135

To make special use of a print, Catherine Anthony divided the center square. Her variation is on page 37.

FAMOUS QUILTERS TALK ABOUT STYLE

Jane Blair is a frequent contributor to *Quilter's Newsletter Magazine* and has had her quilts on five QNM covers. She has taught design and quiltmaking in the Philadelphia area for many years. Jane seldom uses solids or unusual textures, but she includes in her quilts almost anything else--as she says, "anything that works." Jane makes a quilt drawing, which she colors on a tissue overlay. She changes this until it suits her. Jane has no color scheme in mind at this stage. By trial and error she arrives at her final colored plan. Jane adheres strictly to this plan as she translates the drawing into fabrics. She auditions each patch on a design wall, striving first to match the color in her drawing, but also considering the scale of the print.

Georgia Bonesteel is the author of several books, including *Lap Quilting with Georgia Bonesteel* and *More Lap Quilting.* She is well known for her public television series on quilting. Georgia often uses solids to show off the quilting stitch. She uses geometrics and large prints. Her quilts seldom include decorator prints, multicolored prints or unusual textures. Georgia says, "In order to share and pass on a knowledge of quiltmaking, I have found it necessary to draw from many areas and not 'cubby-hole' myself in any one specific direction. Therefore, I try new ideas with our standard patterns.... Over the years I have found my taste, interest and challenges have deviated, adding spark to my quiltmaking."

Moneca Calvert was the Grand Prize winner of the Great American Quilt Festival contest in 1986. Many of her quilts have appeared in magazines. Moneca always uses solids, and she often includes multicolored prints, large prints, decorator prints, and stripes or plaids in her quilts. She especially likes to use unusual fabrics. Moneca says, "I do as little preliminary planning as I can get away with.... Each project is worked on a white felt wall. The pieces are all up there before I start sewing."

Sharyn Craig was named Quilt Teacher of the Year by *The Professional Quilter* magazine in 1985. She is a frequent contributor to *Traditional Quilter* magazine. Sharyn's quilts always include scraps or many fabrics. They are often bright, seldom dark, and never grayed. She seldom uses solids or small calicoes. Sharyn gets her inspiration for quilts mainly from pictures of antique quilts. She is most interested in what she can do differently, how she can depart from this traditional starting point. She challenges herself to create a new, personal statement with each quilt.

Susan Ennis was a designer and artist for *Quilter's Newsletter Magazine* for ten years. She is now designing fabric for apparel. Susan prepares a black, white, and gray value sketch of the block and quilt, then works out the details of color placement as she makes the quilt. She often uses small calicoes, tone-on-tone prints, large prints, and decorator prints; seldom stripes or plaids. Susan says, "I like areas of much blending to play off of areas of high contrast." This, Susan feels, results in a block or quilt that is interesting from a distance as well as close up.

Marianne Fons is the author of *Fine Feathers* and co-author of *Let's Make Waves,* among other books. Marianne says, "I usually make a line drawing on graph paper, a 'map' of a quilt, since I just can't work successfully by the seat of my pants. I never color the sketch in because I find pencils or pens just don't look anything like the fabrics I have. I write in the colors I plan to use and then change them if what I planned doesn't look right. I think that, as you go along, you have to be receptive to a quilt, and give it what it's asking for in terms of color."

Helen Young Frost is the co-author of five books, including *The Lone Star Quilt Handbook* and *The Flying Geese Quilt.* Helen usually starts with fabrics in mind, drawing her color scheme from the colors in the prints. She makes a color sketch of the block and often makes changes as the quilt progresses. She carefully considers placement of each fabric. Helen always uses small calicoes, tone-on-tone prints, multicolored prints, and large prints; seldom solids, stripes or plaids. Helen says, "I mostly love florals! I just can't help it! I know I should use different types, but I have to like the fabric all by itself before I'll buy it."

Harriet Hargrave is the author of *Heirloom Machine Quilting.* She is a shopowner and nationally known teacher of machine quilting. Harriet usually starts with fabrics in mind. She prepares color sketches of the block and quilt and auditions patches for a prototype block on a design wall. She often deviates from her plan as the quilt progresses. She most often uses scraps or many fabrics, including solids, stripes, plaids, geometrics, tone-on-tone prints, and large prints. Harriet says, "I most enjoy recreating antique quilts with today's fabrics and techniques--especially machine quilting intricate designs onto the surface."

Roberta Horton is the author of several books, including *An Amish Adventure* and *Plaids & Stripes.* She has designed several collections of plaid and striped fabrics, as well as prints. Her quilts are always scrap quilts, and they always include plaids or stripes. She often uses large prints and geometrics; seldom small calicoes or tone-on-tone prints. Roberta usually begins the design process with fabrics in mind. She works out the details of color placement as she makes the quilt, auditioning patches on a design wall. Roberta says, "I seem to be most interested in the fabric selection part of quiltmaking. The real turn-on seems to be 'What will this piece of fabric look like cut-up?' And then, 'What will it look like placed next to these other fabrics?' "

Helen Kelley is the author of *Scarlet Ribbons* and *Guidelines for Dating Quilts.* Her "Loose Threads" column appears monthly in *Quilter's Newsletter Magazine.* Helen's quilts always include solids; often small calicoes. She seldom uses large prints, decorator prints, or unusual textures. Helen consciously applies color theory, and prepares color sketches of block and quilt. She auditions each patch on a design wall, carefully considering its placement.

Nancy Martin is the president of That Patchwork Place, Inc., and author of ten books, including *Pieces of the Past* and *Back to Square One*. Her quilts are always Scrap Quilts that include stripes, plaids, large prints, and geometrics. Nancy never uses solids. She usually begins the design process with fabrics or a color scheme in mind. She never makes a sketch or consciously applies color theory. After initial sorting, Nancy quickly considers placement of each color family, and she randomly places each fabric in the designated area for that color family.

Mary Mashuta is the author of *Wearable Art for Real People*. She makes story quilts about events from her life, and she is currently working on a book about these quilts. Mary uses color and printed fabric to tell her story. She often collects fabric for a particular quilt over an extended period of time. Mary works out the details of color placement as she makes the quilt. Mary says,"I'm not locked into a system; my quilts don't look like they come out of the same mold. I do whatever is necessary colorwise and designwise to tell my story."

Marsha McCloskey is the author of nine books, including *Small Quilts* and *Lessons in Machine Piecing*. Marsha's quilts always include stripes and plaids, small calicoes, tone-on-tone prints, multicolored prints, and large prints. Most of her quilts are Scrap Quilts. Marsha begins by making a value sketch of the quilt. She selects a range of fabric for each color. At this point, Marsha assembles patches for a portion of the quilt on a design wall to work out the details. Marsha says, "A quilt in progress needs constant reevaluation. I don't, however, let the endless possibilities and decisions paralyze me. At some point, I just sew the top together and get on with it."

Liz Porter is the co-author of *Classic Basket Patterns* and *Let's Make Waves,* among other books. She is also a craft editor for Better Homes and Gardens Books. Liz uses many fabrics with a traditional flavor, such as tone-on-tone prints, stripes, plaids, and geometrics. She always starts with a preliminary sketch to work out the values or the colors. Liz says, "In scrap quilts, I prefer to choose a general batch of fabrics that I want to use and then use them quite randomly in the quilt. I feel quilts can be overplanned and overmanipulated and, therefore, loose their spontaneity. I like quilts to create a life of their own."

Marie Shirer is senior editor of *Quilter's Newsletter Magazine* and the author of *Quilt Settings: A Workbook*. Marie's quilts are predominantly bright and always include multicolored prints and large prints. She seldom uses small calicoes and tone-on-tone prints and never limits herself to just a few fabrics. She makes a black, white, and gray value sketch of the block and quilt, and works out the color details as she makes the quilt. After initial sorting, Marie randomly places each fabric in a scrap quilt.

Ami Simms is the author of *Every Trick in the Book* and *How to Improve Your Quilting Stitch.* She is also a contributing editor to *QUILT* magazine. Ami's quilts are often made from scraps or many fabrics. Her favorite colors are intense, deep hues; she never uses stripes or plaids or unusual textures. Ami says, "I'm going nuts with hand-dyed solids and mottled fabrics now. I almost hate to work with commercially made stuff."

Doreen Speckmann is a well-known teacher and lecturer whose quilts have appeared in a number of quilting magazines. Doreen's recent quilts are predominantly bright and made from scraps. She always includes tone-on-tone prints, multicolored prints and large prints; seldom solids. Doreen starts with a design on graph paper. She sometimes colors the drawing, but she is more likely to work out the colors on a design wall. Doreen says, "What I try to avoid is over-intellectualizing about fabric choices... I've learned to listen to my instincts."

Helen Squire is the author of *Dear Helen, Can You Tell Me...All About Quilting Designs,* and *Ask Helen, More About Quilting Designs*. She writes a regular column in *Lady's Circle Patchwork Quilts.* Helen begins each project with a theme, choosing the pattern by its name. She works from a color sketch of the quilt. Her quilts always include solids to allow an open area for quilting. She often uses small calicoes and large prints; seldom decorator prints. Helen says, "I select the colors, make a worksheet, figure yardage, then go looking for what I need to buy. I do *not* save fabric.... I normally have no trouble finding what I need."

Louise O. Townsend is a long-time quiltmaker and managing editor of *Quilter's Newsletter Magazine*. Louise begins a quilting project with a black, white, and gray value sketch of the quilt and a color sketch of the block. Her quilts always include solids and bright colors. She often uses small calicoes; seldom large prints, and never decorator prints. Louise says, "My style is distinctly eclectic.... Whatever the design, every quilt has some special meaning, usually to the recipient. It may be the name of the pattern, particular colors, style, or whatever."

Blanche Young is the co-author of several books, including *Lone Star Quilt Handbook* and *Trip Around the World Quilts*. She consciously applies color theory in her quilt planning. Blanche works out the details of color placement as she makes the quilt, randomly placing each fabric after the initial sorting. Her quilts always include large prints, decorator prints, and unusual textures. Blanche says, "I love working with many colors or shades of color. I have decided I am a 'flowery' person--avoiding stripes and checks. I love blending the mediums and darks together."

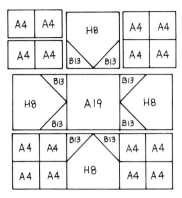

Quilter's Dream, B29, 12", pg. 135

Cut the H and A patches from a large print. It is not necessary to position the print in any special way.

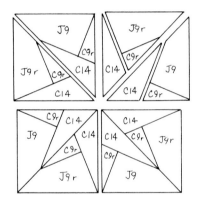

Carnival Ride, C24, 12", pg. 135

Press all seams toward the C14 patches to oppose perfectly at the block center. Press the final seam open.

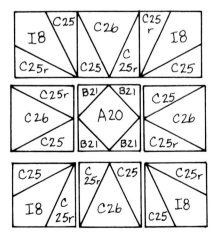

Sweethearts' Star, C52, 9", page 135

Press seam allowances away from the I patches and the C26 patches to permit you to make crisp points.

The block at the right is from the large Quilter's Dream quilt on page 83. The block at the far right is from the small quilt segment. The large quilt is made from scraps carefully sorted. As there is so much going on in terms of colors and pattern, the range of each color is narrow. A single block does not look scrappy, but each block is made from a different set of fabrics. The block from the second version looks similar to the first block. However, all blocks are made from the same few fabrics in the small quilt. The large quilt looks old-fashioned in its colorful scrappiness. The small one looks more contemporary. The soft, watercolor print and the blending solids have a very different look from the busy prints in the large quilt.

This is a simple block that looks quite different in the two styles shown at right. The first block is from the large version of the Carnival Ride Quilt on page 85. The block at the far right is from the small quilt segment. In the large quilt, scraps in many colors provide the interest. Color placement varies from one block to another. For continuity, each block has the same plain background. Print patches are paired with coordinating solids for definition and relief. The block at the far right relies on special use of striped and printed fabrics for interest. Only three fabrics are used in the block. The background uses a border stripe to frame the block. Triangles are cut from precisely the same part of a large print for a kaleidoscopic effect. Each block utilizes a different part of the print.

The block at the right is from the large version of Sweethearts' Star on page 93. The block at the far right is from the small quilt segment. In the large quilt, the overall design looks somewhat complex, so I chose scraps to be quite uniform. A broader range might have made the pattern less coherent. To ensure that the rings would be perfectly evident, I used the same pink print throughout the quilt. The smaller quilt segment is made from just a few fabrics. Because the scraps range so little in color and value in the large example, the lack of scraps in the small version accounts for very little of the difference between the two quilts. The placement of lights, mediums, and darks is different in the two versions, and this creates the biggest change in the overall effect.

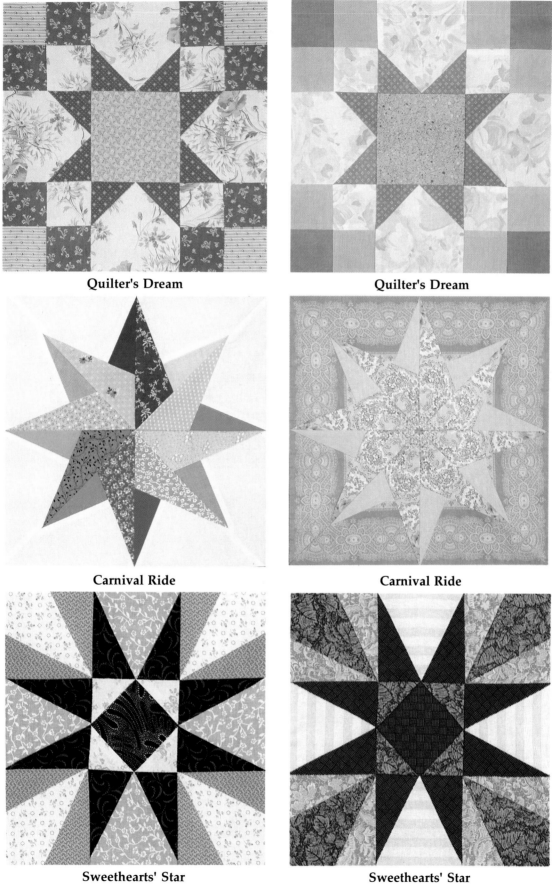

Quilter's Dream

Quilter's Dream

Carnival Ride

Carnival Ride

Sweethearts' Star

Sweethearts' Star

Marching Band

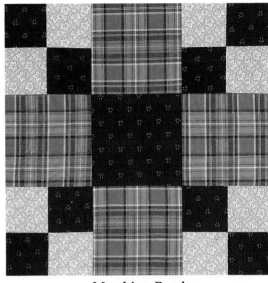

Marching Band

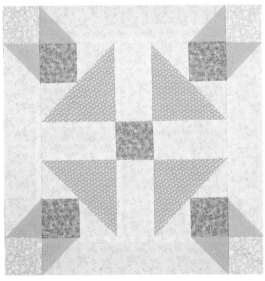

Rabbit's Foot, trad.

Rabbit's Foot, trad.

Picnic in the Park

Picnic in the Park

At the far left is the block from the large Marching Band quilt on page 92. At the left is the block from the small quilt segment. The color schemes are different, but the placement of light and dark is similar in the two examples. The large quilt is made from scraps, whereas the small one has just a few fabrics. In this pattern, the overall design is more important than the individual block. In order to create uniformity throughout the large quilt, each block is scrappy, with a variety of red prints and white prints. For focus, the light blue patches are all the same in one block, though they vary from block to block. The pattern is simple, and the color scheme offers plenty of latitude, so fabrics in each color category may be interpreted broadly.

At the far left is the block from the large Rabbit's Foot quilt on page 84. The block from the quilt segment is at the left. The colors in the large quilt are pale and feminine. The prints are fluid, soft, and delicately floral. Some of the prints are quite large, with the patches cut from various parts of the print, randomly. Each block in this quilt is made from a different set of fabrics. Color and value placement varies from block to block. However, the color scheme is constant throughout the quilt. The second version has darker, more masculine colors. The warm background gives the block an antique look. Plaids and a stripe lend orderly definition. In this quilt, a secondary pattern emerges at the junctures between blocks. The repeated fabrics and narrower sashes enhance this effect.

At the far left is a block from the large Picnic in the Park quilt on page 94. At the near left is a block from the small quilt segment. This is a busy pattern with a busy pieced sashing arrangement. Ordinarily, I might shy away from using many colors or many scrap fabrics in such a quilt, but I like the activity here. Busy, multicolored prints in a variety of colors make a lively quilt. To focus attention on the blocks, each block has a different color scheme. Then, to tie all of the blocks together, the pieced sashes are uniformly scrappy. In contrast, the small quilt segment is made from only two fabrics, a solid and print that reads as a solid. The busyness in this example comes from the bright color and the strong contrast. The two-color version has a flat, two-dimensional quality.

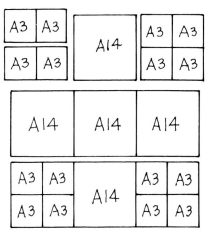

Marching Band, A37, 9", pg. 135

This is among the easiest of blocks. Press seam allowances to opposite sides to help you match joints.

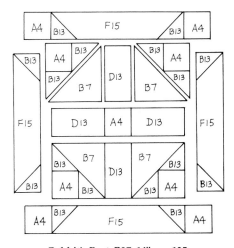

Rabbit's Foot, B27, 14", pg. 135

Press seam allowances toward the D rectangles for sharp, smooth points on the triangles.

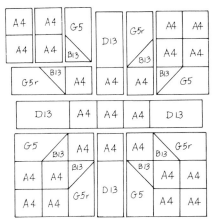

Picnic in the Park, B33, 14", pg. 135

Lay out patches for a block on the table. Spread them into rows to help you see the piecing sequence.

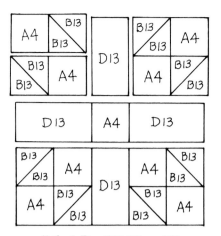

Father's Day, B42, 10", pg. 136

This block is suitable for setting with Granny's Trunk alternate blocks or with pieced sashes.

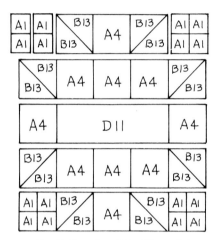

Family Reunion, B62, 10", pg. 136

Join A1's into four-patch units and join pairs of B13's into squares before assembling the parts into a block.

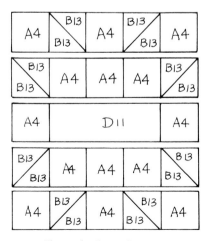

Fireworks, B45, 10", pg. 136

Take care to keep all of the signatures right side up when you join the blocks into a quilt.

At the right is the block from the large Father's Day quilt on page 91. The block from the small quilt segment is at the far right. The large quilt is made from scraps in a black/dark brown, gold/tan, teal, and cream color scheme. In each block, the colors are placed the same way. Fabrics are sorted into color categories and placed almost randomly within the defined area for that color. This treatment obscures the block boundaries and emphasizes the overall pattern. Many of the prints are busy ones. The simple pattern and color scheme lend themselves to a lively use of scraps. Each color in the quilt is interpreted broadly. In the small quilt segment, just two solid fabrics are used. The counterchange of light and dark creates an interesting, but uncomplicated, look.

The block at the right is from the Family Reunion quilt on page 111. The block at the far right is from Kate's Friendship Sampler on page 97. Both of the blocks are incorporated in Scrap Quilts. In the Family Reunion quilt, each block is scrappy, with many colors and fabrics; in the sampler, each block is made from just a few colors and fabrics. The sampler block is made from dainty florals in pastel tints. It has a sweet and gentle style. The other block is made from deep, rich colors with strong contrasts. The prints include many geometrics with crisp, clean lines. Each block has a number of colors. The same background fabric and accent fabrics throughout the quilt lend continuity. In the Sampler Quilt, the same muslin center in each block provides the continuity.

The block at the right is from the Fireworks quilt segment on page 111. At the far right is the same block from Kate's Friendship Sampler on page 97. Compare these blocks with Family Reunion, above. The two block patterns are quite similar, but the styles are very different. The block from the Fireworks quilt is made from a few bright prints in a patriotic theme. The brightness is toned down by the use of a darker-than-usual background solid. The block from Kate's Sampler is made from delicate floral prints in soft colors. Just a few fabrics are included in a single block, but the quilt has many different scraps. The value placement is similar in both Fireworks blocks, but the contrasts are subtler in the sampler version.

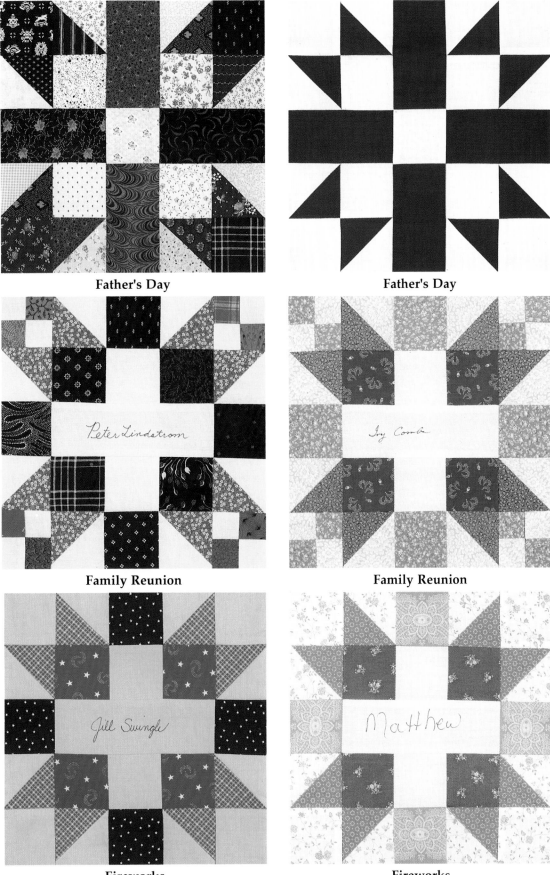

Father's Day

Father's Day

Family Reunion

Family Reunion

Fireworks

Fireworks

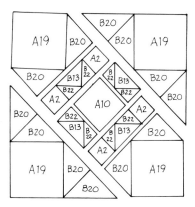

Pride of Iowa, C33, 12", pg. 136

The small star's background can match the large star points or block background, or it can be a third fabric.

Pride of Iowa, Aileen Taylor

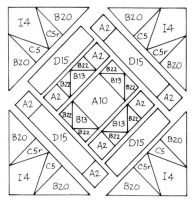

Thorny Crown, C45, 12", pg. 136

Colors can be crisp or soft; when the rectangles match the background, an interesting hole appears in the star.

Thorny Crown, Wilma Rozendaal

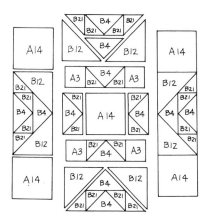

Colorado Star, C53, 12", pg. 136

Delicate and floral or bold and patriotic, this pattern looks entirely transformed with different fabrics.

Colorado Star, Shirley Wegert

Pride of Iowa, Linda Olivier

Pride of Iowa, Sharon K. Jolly

Thorny Crown, Leona Vande Voort

Thorny Crown, Linda Olivier

Colorado Star, Rosemary Angelos

Colorado Star, Shirley Wegert

Piecemaker's Block, Etsuko Furusawa

Piecemaker's Block, Ikuyo Saito

Green Gables, Cheri Spoelstra

Green Gables, Aileen Taylor

Hudson Bay Block, Aileen Taylor

Hudson Bay Block, Diane Myers

Colors and fabrics can take this block from the sweet, fresh style of Etsuko Furusawa's block to the handsome sophistication of Ikuyo Saito's block. Etsuko's block has delicate florals and pastel solids with a darker accent for the center star. She cut the diamonds carefully to center a printed motif. The block is basically mono-chromatic. Ikuyo's block combines solids and mid-sized florals with strong linear patterns. The stripes, checks and plaids give the block a masculine appearance. Her block is principally neutral. The color accents are provided by the red and yellow figures in the prints and plaid. The patterned fabrics are fairly bold; the subtle colors, the blending shades, and the inclusion of three solids provide relief. See two more versions of this block on page 58.

The placement of values is quite different in the two blocks at the left. Different shapes emerge where patches match the background. In Cheri's block, some of the small squares match the background, bringing out the chain of navy squares. In Aileen's block, the center square matches the background, piercing the star and emphasizing the ring. Cheri's colors are strong and her prints crisp. The plaid, pin dot, and large floral all have neatly defined edges. The tawny background solid gives her block an antique appearance. Aileen's prints are fluid, mostly delicate florals. Two of the prints have feathery, fine detailing in the backgrounds. Aileen's dark green background is a departure from the softness, defining the shapes.

Both of these blocks include areas of strong contrast. Both include florals, prints that read as solids, multicolored prints, and rhythmic prints. Even the color schemes are similar, with beige, cream, and blue-gray in each block. The principal difference between the blocks is in the value placement. Aileen Taylor's block has a dark background behind a light star. All 24 star points are light. Diane Myers' block has a light background behind the stars. Eight of the star points are light and four are medium values. In her block, the square patches are all the same dark print, encircling the center star. These squares vary in color and value in Aileen's block. In general, Aileen's fabrics are a little more tone-on-tone and have crisper details. Diane's fabrics have more movement, but softer edges.

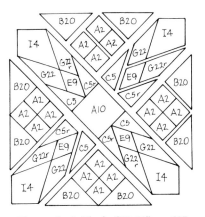

Piecemaker's Block, C49, 12", pg. 135

This block is attractive set with plain sashes. Press seam allowances toward the center for perfect joints.

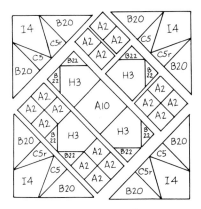

Green Gables, C49, 12", pg. 136

Cut the B20 triangles with the long edge on the straight grain to stabilize the block's edges.

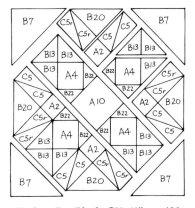

Hudson Bay Block, C53, 12", pg. 136

Careful cutting and accurate seam allowances will assure perfect points.

FROM BLOCKS TO QUILTS

In the last chapter, we discussed style possibilities related to the quilt block. Another very big consideration is the arrangement of the blocks in the quilt. The arrangement is called the set, and there are many different sets from which to choose.

Blocks can be set with sashing strips between them and setting squares where the sashes intersect; they can be sewn side by side; or they can be set in a checkerboard of alternating plain and pieced blocks. In any of these three basic sets, the blocks can be arranged in horizontal and vertical rows or the blocks can be set on point, with the rows running diagonally across the quilt. This makes six basic sets.

These basic sets are just the beginning, though. By adding to the equation pieced sashes, pieced setting squares, and pieced alternate blocks, we greatly expand the possibilities for new and exciting quilt designs.

Plain sashes and alternate blocks serve to define or frame the blocks and to organize them in a pleasing, structured way. In contrast, pieced sashes or pieced alternate blocks tie the blocks together, obscuring their boundaries and creating secondary patterns.

Sashes and alternate blocks, whether plain or pieced, often have larger patches and are simpler than the quilt blocks that they accompany. Therefore, they offer a measure of relief and a change of rhythm from the blocks. Some of the larger patches provide space for elegant quilting motifs, as well.

Several of the quilts in this book were made with pieced sets. Marching Band on page 92 has pieced sashes and pieced setting squares; Picnic in the Park (page 94), Quilter's Dream (page 83), and Father's Day (page 91) have pieced sashes; Sweethearts' Star (page 93), Family Reunion (page 111), Fireworks (page 111), and Quilter's Dream (page 83) have pieced alternate blocks.

Study these quilts to see how the piecing in the sash or alternate block relates to the block. Blocks and pieced setting units generally share similar patches or block divisions, and the pieced units complete or expand on the patterns established in the blocks.

Many pieced sashes, setting squares, and alternate blocks are shown on pages 74-81. Full-size patterns for these and for plain sashes and alternate blocks are at the back of the book. In order to choose a pieced sash or alternate block to suit your chosen block, trace or photocopy the desired coloring book blocks and assemble enough of them to judge the effect.

OPTIONS FOR SETTING BLOCKS IN A QUILT

1. Blocks set side by side in straight rows.	6. Blocks set with pieced sashes in diagonal rows.
2. Blocks set side by side in diagonal rows.	7. Blocks set with alternate blocks in straight rows.
3. Blocks set with plain sashes in straight rows.	8. Blocks set straight with pieced alternate blocks.
4. Blocks set with pieced sashes in straight rows.	9. Blocks set diagonally with alternate blocks.
5. Blocks set with plain sashes in diagonal rows.	10. Blocks set diagonally with pieced alternate blocks.

For blocks set side by side, the blocks are sewn together edge to edge to make straight rows. Then the rows of blocks are joined edge to edge.

For sashed sets, sashes match the block in length and they match the setting square in width. Patterns for sashes are on pages 187-192. Patterns A1, A3, A4, A7, and A14 on pages 154-157 would make appropriate setting squares. One sashing strip is sewn between each two blocks. An extra sash is sewn to the block end. Whole rows are made of blocks separated by strips. Sash rows are also made by joining sashes end to end with setting squares between them. Block rows are then joined with sash rows between them. An extra sash row is sewn to each end of the quilt to complete the quilt top.

For alternate block sets, you will need plain squares the same size as the blocks. Patterns for these plain squares are on pages 187-191. You will have one more block than you have plain squares. These plain squares are sewn between blocks in a checkerboard pattern. Blocks are sewn to plain squares to make rows. The first row has a block, then a plain square, then a block, and so on, ending with a block. The second row starts and ends with a plain square. Rows are joined to complete the quilt.

In a diagonal set, the rows run from corner to corner of the quilt, rather than from side to side. Individual rows for a diagonally set quilt look just like rows for a straight set, with blocks joined edge to edge, except that each row ends with two large triangles. Whereas these rows are all the same length in a straight-set quilt, the rows vary in length in a diagonally set quilt.

In order to sew blocks side by side in a diagonal set, arrange the blocks on the floor, placing each at an angle with the corners of the blocks at the top, bottom, and sides of the quilt. Notice how the blocks are in rows that run diagonally across the quilt. Blocks are joined edge to edge, with the first row (at one corner of the quilt) having just one block. The second row has three blocks sewn edge to edge. The third row has five blocks, and so on, with each row progressively longer. Rows taper again, getting shorter and shorter, as you approach the opposite corner of the quilt. When you have your blocks arranged on the floor, you can spread the blocks apart between rows before sewing them. This will help you see the rows. In order to square off the edges of the quilt, you will need to add large triangles, half the size of the block. For the quilt's corners, you will need triangles one-fourth the size of the block. These triangles are sewn to the ends of the rows before the rows are joined.

To make the patterns for edge triangles, trace the pattern for the square that matches the block size. Rule a diagonal from one corner to the opposite corner of the square, forming two triangles. To one of the triangles, add a quarter-inch seam allowance outside the diagonal to complete a template. For the corner triangle, trace the square again. Rule two diagonals, crossing at the center of the square, to form four triangles. Add seam allowances to the two short edges of one triangle to make a pattern template.

Diagonal sets can also include sashes or alternate blocks. Individual rows are made just as you would make them for a straight set, with blocks' edges sewn to sashes or alternate plain squares. Lay out the blocks and the other patches on the floor, being sure to include the edge and corner triangles. Spread the blocks and patches into diagonal rows to see how to sew them together. For sashed sets, you will need small triangles half the size of the setting squares at the ends of the sash rows. Appropriate patterns for these triangles are B10, B12, B13, and B21 on pages 160-162.

JOINING YOUR BLOCKS INTO A QUILT TOP

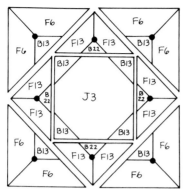

Mother Nature Block, E29, 12", pg. 136

This is the perfect alternate block for Covered Bridge, Dutch Boy, or other blocks with corners to match these.

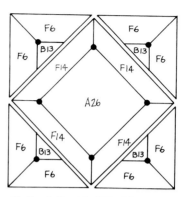

Coffee & Danish, E17, 12", pg. 136

Try setting this block alternately with Sunday's Child for a unique quilt.

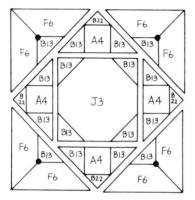

Around the World in 80 Days, E33, 12", pg. 136

Here's a pieced alternate block that would make a pretty quilt on its own. The corner triangles are set in.

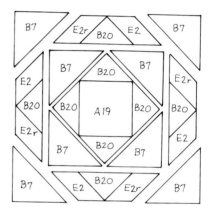

Moondance, C25, 12", pg. 136

This creates a handsome secondary pattern when set alternately with A Stitch in Time.

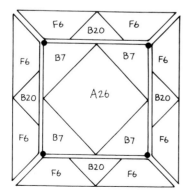

Heat Wave, E17, 12", pg. 136

Make the center square from a solid fabric in order to show off fine quilting.

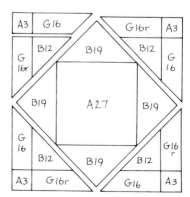

String of Pearls, B21, 12", pg. 136

This block is lovely alternated with Blue Bayou or with almost any block made with A3 patches.

Mother Nature Block

Coffee & Danish

Around the World in Eighty Days

Moondance, Diane Myers

Heat Wave

String of Pearls

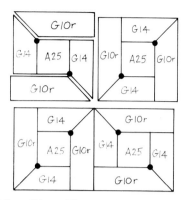

A Long Way to Tipperary, E20, 12", pg. 136

This block set alternately with State Fair (reversed) forms an interesting secondary pattern.

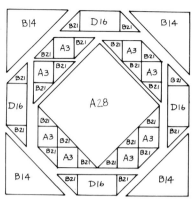

Williamsburg Block, C41, 12", pg. 137

This block pairs perfectly with Purple Mountain Majesties or Strawberry Fields.

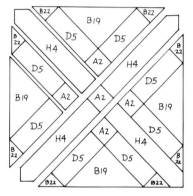

Gone Fishing, C29, 12", pg. 137

This block completes the cross motifs when set alternately with Shropshire Lad or Wednesday's Child.

A4	A4	D13	A4	A4
A4	A4	D13	A4	A4
D13	D13	A19	D13	D13
A4	A4	D13	A4	A4
A4	A4	D13	A4	A4

Over the Rainbow, A25, 12", pg. 137

This block looks good set alternately with Quilter's Dream or Thorny Crown.

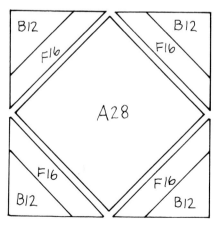

Wedding Band, B16, 9", pg. 137

This block was made for Sweethearts Star. It could be set attractively with Marching Band, as well.

A Long Way to Tipperary

Williamsburg Block

Gone Fishing

Over the Rainbow

Wedding Band

Wedding Band

Sugar Bowl

Sugar Bowl

Cotton Patch

China Plate

Tapestry

Nantucket

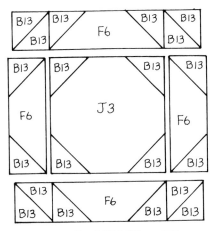

Sugar Bowl, B36, 10", pg. 137

This block, when paired with Family Reunion or Fire-works, forms a fascinating overall pattern.

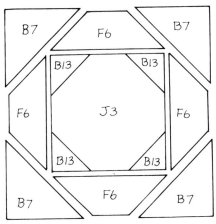

Cotton Patch, B19, 10", pg. 137

This block pairs perfectly with Home for the Holidays. The octagon provides extra space for favorite sayings.

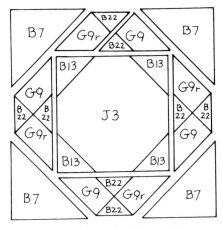

China Plate, C36, 10", pg. 137

Set this block alternately with April Love or one of the 10" signature patches for a unique quilt.

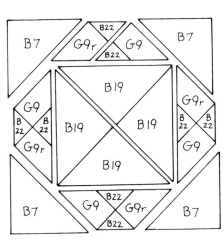

Tapestry, C35, 10", pg. 137

The block center makes good use of a striped motif. Set Tapestry blocks with Best of Friends or Back to School.

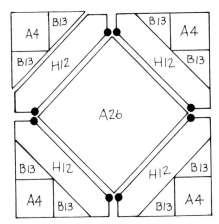

Nantucket, E25, 10", pg. 137

This block fits beautifully alongside many 10" blocks. Try it with Wilderness Trail for a striking quilt.

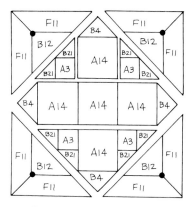

Country Life, E33, 12", pg. 137

Country Life is ideal set alternately with Sorority Block or with other designs with similar corners.

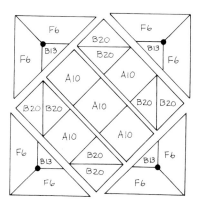

Dutch Boy, E25, 12", pg. 137

Dutch Boy looks good set alternately with blocks having similar corners, such as Wabash Cannonball.

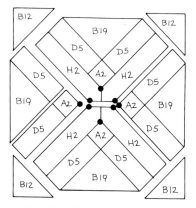

The River Bank, E24, 12", pg. 137

This block makes an interesting counterpart to Mexican Star variations such as A Summer Place.

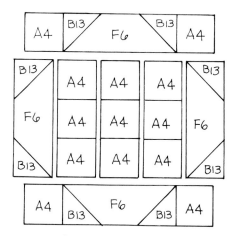

Cat Nap, B36, 10", pg. 137

Cat Nap set alternately with Hometown Hero makes an interesting all-over pattern.

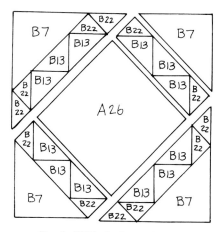

Goodwill Block, C42, 10", pg. 137

Set this block alternately with Heart of Gold for an easy, but intricate-looking quilt.

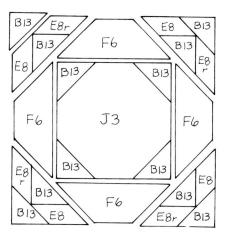

Granny's Trunk, B36, 10", pg. 137

This alternate block makes a delightful complement to Father's Day or many of the 10" signature blocks.

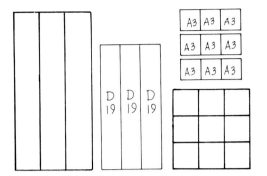

Pieced Sash & Setting Square for 9" Blocks

This is the sash and setting square combination used in the Marching Band quilt and segment on page 92.

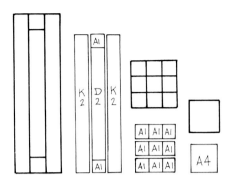

Pieced Sash & Setting Squares for 10" Blocks

This sash makes a small Trip Around the World motif when combined with the nine-patch setting square.

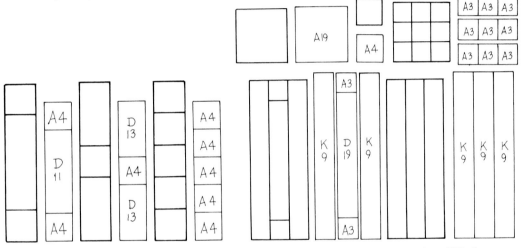

More Pieced Sashes for 10" Blocks

The pieced sash at the left is the one used in the Father's Day quilt and quilt segment shown on page 91.

Pieced Sashes & Setting Squares for 12" Blocks

These two sashes make interesting secondary patterns when set with the nine-patch setting square.

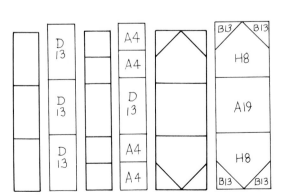

More Pieced Sashes for 12" Blocks

The block at the left was used in the Quilter's Dream quilt and the segment shown at the bottom of page 83.

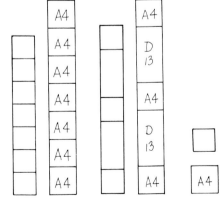

Pieced Sashes & Setting Square for 14" Blocks

The pieced sash on the left was used to make the Picnic in the Park quilt and small segment on page 94.

SCRAPS & SCRAP QUILTS

Everyone loves a Scrap Quilt. Each print seems to have a story of its own, and the mix of prints tells so much about the time in which the quilt was made. Scrap Quilts made today will be treasured years hence for their glimpse into the past. Scrap fabrics add nuances of color, shading, and visual texture that give depth and richness to a quilt.

For quilters like me, who revel in quilt planning and color selection but get bogged down in the routine of actually making the quilt, Scrap Quilts offer the opportunity of extending our enjoyment all through the process. With a scrap quilt, you're never done with the planning until the quilt top is entirely finished!

First, you choose a pattern. Next you'll need to plan which colors to include and how far each color should range. Then you'll select fabrics and sort them by color or value. You'll decide where to place the colors in the block (and whether or not each block will be the same in this regard).

As you sew, you'll constantly be making little decisions about which fabrics to put next to each other. After the blocks are completed, you'll need to plan the best sequence of blocks across the quilt surface, taking into account the color balance.

Some quilters "audition" each patch on a design wall. Most don't agonize over every little decision, though. Usually, a quick and easy judgment will do. Even if you plan to be completely random about it, I think you will find yourself sometimes vetoing patch combinations and looking for something more suitable. After all, this is your quilt, and you want it to be just so. Every decision makes your quilt a little more of a personal statement. Every choice you make affects the whole. Every detail that you consider (and some that you don't even think about) becomes a thread in the intricate weave of the quilt surface.

Every small detail that you think through is there in your quilt to give pleasure to anyone who cares to look closely. The way you peppered your quilt with a few colors just a little brighter than the rest; the new shapes that suggest themselves where adjacent patches blend a little more than usual; the lovely pairing of two unlikely prints; the unique way you interpreted colors and made use of prints--all layer the quilt with a delightful complexity just inviting exploration and awaiting discovery.

Any design can be made into a Scrap Quilt. In this book alone, you will find examples of Scrap Quilts made from all types of patterns.

DESIGN OPTIONS FOR SCRAP QUILTS

1. Distinct blocks set with sashing (pg. 84)
2. Two-block patterns (pg. 93)
3. All-over designs (pg. 94)
4. Log Cabin Quilts (pg. 121)
5. Sampler Quilts (pg. 112)
6. Friendship Quilts (pg. 97)

Simple patterns fairly cry out for scraps. Compare the two versions of Marching Band on page 92. Complex patterns can also be made from scraps, although they can be equally pleasant in just a few fabrics. (Compare the two Sweethearts' Star quilts on page 93.) There are many ways of incorporating scraps into your quilt. Scraps can be chosen from a color scheme with a block emphasis (Rabbit's Foot, page 84) or with an overall emphasis (Father's Day, page 91). The scraps can be multicolored (Carnival Ride, page 85) or a whole range of colors can be used (Smoky Mountain Log Cabin, page 121). For a more complex design, scraps will add busyness, so you'll want to keep other design elements less busy. Observe the style considerations discussed in the Block Style chapter.

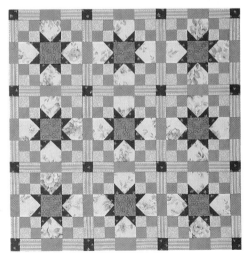

Quilter's Dream, 74" x 88", original quilt designed and made by Judy Martin, 1989. This is a scrap quilt in a red, blue, pink, green, and white color scheme drawn from the border fabric. The various colors are placed identically in each block. Each patch of the same color within a block is cut from the same fabric, but each block uses a different set of fabrics. The pieced sashes and setting squares remain the same throughout the quilt. The design is moderately simple; the interest comes from the large number of colors used. To keep the quilt from becoming too busy, fabrics are sorted in a very limited range for each color.

Quilter's Dream quilt segment (top right), 36" x 36". The same block is set alternately with a pieced alternate block that complements it. This arrangement of Quilter's Dream and Over the Rainbow blocks forms an appealing secondary pattern of chains.

Quilter's Dream quilt segment (bottom right), 44" x 44". This version has the same block and set as the large version. The colors are a little different, and just a few fabrics are used.

Quilter's Dream block photos/diagrams, 62-63; Over the Rainbow, 76-77; coloring book blocks, 135, 137; quilt instructions, 143.

Rabbit's Foot, 97" x 97", traditional design made by Judy Martin, 1988. Scraps in rose, blue, and cream are used to create blocks that share a color scheme yet look quite different from each other. Each block stands alone, separated from the others by wide, plain sashes. Fabrics used for one block are not repeated in other blocks, and the placement of the lights and darks varies from block to block, as well. The quilt becomes an interesting exercise in a theme and variations.

Rabbit's Foot quilt segment, 34" x 34". In this version only a few fabrics are used to make a quilt of identical, repeating blocks. There is a comfortable rhythm to this kind of repetition. Although this is the same set as the larger version, here, a secondary pattern emerges where the blocks interact with the sashes. The repeating colors and fabrics enhance this effect.

Rabbit's Foot block photos and diagram are on pages 64-65. Coloring book block is on page 135. Instructions for the quilt in both versions are on page 143.

Carnival Ride, 65" x 79", original quilt designed and made by Judy Martin, 1990. A simple block in a plain sashed setting gets pizzazz from the use of bright scraps. Color placement varies from block to block; the same muslin background throughout lends continuity.

Carnival Ride quilt segment, 30" x 30". The same block and set is interpreted in just a few fabrics. Stripes and prints are cut for special effect.

Block photos and diagrams, pages 62-63; coloring book block, 135; quilt instructions, 144.

Covered Bridge

State Fair

Hayride

Double Nine-Patch, trad.

Peace on Earth

Cut Glass Dish, trad.

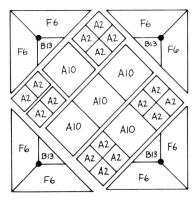

Covered Bridge, E33, 12", pg. 138

Frame each scrappy block with the same striped fabric, and set with sashes for a handsome quilt.

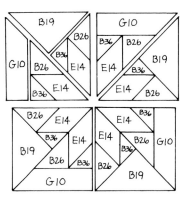

State Fair, C32, 12", pg. 138

The use of different scrap prints in the background patches enlivens this simple block.

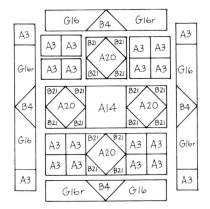

Hayride, C53, 12", pg. 138

Make each block from scraps in the same colors, and set with light red K9 sashes and cream A3 setting squares.

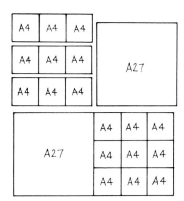

Double Nine-Patch, A20, 12", pg. 138

Join blocks side by side. At the right and bottom edges of the quilt, add a row of half blocks to provide balance.

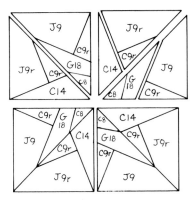

Peace on Earth, C28, 12", pg. 138

Use a different border stripe in each block. The same solid accent will provide continuity.

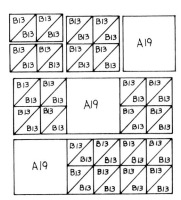

Cut Glass Dish, B51, 12", pg. 138

Use the same range of cream and tan prints for the lights throughout, but vary the darks in each block.

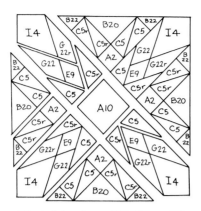

Alice's Adventures, C57, 12", pg. 138

This block, with its many-pointed star, is perfect for scraps in a limited color scheme.

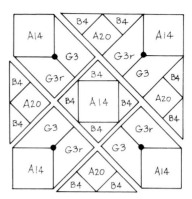

Red Rover, E29, 12", pg. 138

This block is simple in spite of the set-in patches. It makes a lovely multicolored Scrap Quilt.

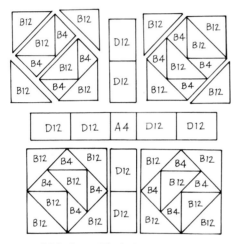

Main Street Block, C36, 14", pg. 138

Consider making blocks from scraps, varying background fabrics and colors from block to block.

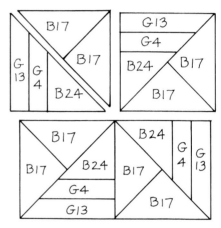

Movie Reel, C29, 10", pg. 138

This perfectly easy block is great for scrap prints with solid accents. Make blocks in many different colors.

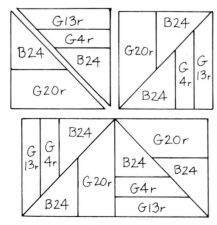

Serendipity, C29, 10", pg. 138

Blocks set side by side create an interesting overall design. Use scraps in a color scheme.

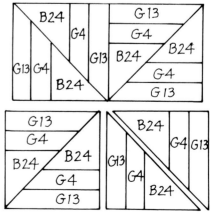

Summer Breeze, C35, 10", pg. 138

Use scraps in many colors to make blocks, each with the same light/dark pattern. Set them side by side.

COLOR & FABRIC IDEAS FOR SCRAP QUILTS

TO ADD INTEREST	TO LEND CONTINUITY
variations in shading, values that shift	flat counterchange of values
wider range within a color	tight range within a color
more colors/all colors	limited color scheme
different value or color placement in each block	same color/value placement in each block
different fabrics for patches of the same color	same accent fabric in each block
different background for each block	same background fabric throughout
scrap sashes, setting squares, or alternate blocks	same sash/alternate block fabric throughout
bold or busy prints	prints that look more uniform or read as solids
color tension, colors that clash	more blocks

No matter what format you use for your Scrap Quilt, the quiltmaking process begins with selecting a palette of fabrics. You will select a color scheme or a range of colors and then pick fabrics in each color or color range needed for the quilt. Include fabrics with a variety of sizes and types of prints: basic dots, stripes, plaids, and other rhythmic geometrics; widely spaced motifs; viney, packed prints; voluptuous florals; soft, watercolor effects; large prints; and tiny calicoes. Stretch a little with your colors. Don't match them too carefully or your quilt won't look like a Scrap Quilt. Every fabric need not be a current favorite. The overall mix is more important than any single fabric.

When you have gathered the fabrics, spread them out in a staggered array to see how they look together. Eliminate any that don't seem to work. Then decide if you have enough fabrics to develop your quilt according to plan.

The number of different fabrics in a Scrap Quilt can vary tremendously. The Scrap Quilts photographed in this book range from one having fewer than 20 fabrics (Ozark Log Cabin, page 122) to one having 200 (Picnic in the Park, page 94). My Scrap Quilts generally average about 100 fabrics. The actual number of fabrics has less to do with how scrappy a quilt looks than you might think. Kate's Friendship Sampler (page 97) has about the same number of fabrics as the Adirondack Log Cabin (page 122). The Log Cabin looks much more uniform, with fewer colors, but it has more nuances of shading than the Sampler Quilt. How scrappy a quilt looks depends on the number of different colors, how uniformly the colors are placed, and how far each color ranges, not just on how many fabrics are included.

I suppose if I had to set a lower limit, I'd say that I prefer Scrap Quilts to have at least 40 fabrics. To my mind, Ozark Log Cabin (page 122) has too few fabrics. It was made for a quilt challenge, and the fabrics were restricted to just a few. Sierra Log Cabin (page 120) has around 40 fabrics, and I wouldn't want any fewer.

When I am making a Scrap Quilt, I don't plan on a certain number of fabrics. The number depends on what I have available. First I plan which colors I intend to use and I pull out all of the appropriate fabrics from my stash. Then, whether or not I have plenty of suitable fabrics, I make a trip to my local quilt shop for additional fabrics in these colors. This improves the mix in the quilt and, even more importantly, it replenishes fabrics even before I use them. The more different fabrics I have, the less of each I must use. When I don't need to use the last little bit of any fabric, the variety in my stash grows, rather than diminishes.

Often, I will adjust my fabric selection according to the cutting requirements. For example, if I have twelve pink prints for Quilter's Dream (page 83), and I need twenty large pink squares, I'll eliminate two of the pink fabrics so I can cut an even two squares from each of 10 fabrics to arrive at the total needed. (Sometimes I might cut two each of 11 fabrics, so I'll have two extra squares to give me some options as I sew the last few blocks.) If I am making a plain Log Cabin (page 119) with 16 blocks, I'll need to cut 16 dark logs from each log length (16 L1, 16 L2, 16 L3, 16 L4, 16 L5, and 16 L6). If I have 30 dark fabrics, I'll see if I can round up two more. Then, from each of 16 of the fabrics, I'll cut one each of L1, L3, and L5. From each of the remaining 16 fabrics, I'll cut one each of L2, L4, and L6.

Obviously, it is helpful to have a stash of fabrics on hand if you plan to make Scrap Quilts. If you try to build a Scrap Quilt from fabrics that you can find at the store at any given moment, you'll end up with a less-than-perfect mix. Too many fabrics will be from overmatched, coordinated lines; you'll have the same prints in several colors; and you may not be able to find some colors at all. Instead of settling for "instant scraps," set out to build up your stash over a period of time, buying when you see something you like, or buying to fill gaps in your collection. Eventually, you will have a fabric collection with depth and variety that will make your quilts sing.

HOW TO BUILD YOUR STASH OF FABRICS FOR SCRAP QUILTS

1. Go on a buying trip when you start a quilt. Replenish fabrics in colors you will be using before you use them all up.

2. Buy whenever you see something you love. It won't be around for long.

3. Buy when you need inspiration. There's nothing like a pile of new fabric to get your creative juices flowing.

4. Buy when the fabric is on sale. There are always prints you like but haven't bought before because of the expense. When they're on sale, all of a sudden they look indispensable.

5. Periodically, make a shopping list of gaps in your collection, and make a special trip to the store just to fill these gaps and round out your collection.

6. Buy extra fabric whenever you make any project. The leftovers will make a great addition to your stash. (When I am starting a project, I like to buy everything that I might consider including. This way, I don't have to make up my mind until I get home. I never mind having bought something that I didn't use right away. It just goes into my stash. I have been known to buy 10 or 15 yards of fabric to make a single 36" quilt!)

7. Buy fabric when you're on vacation. People always seem to budget some extra spending money into their vacations. Fabric makes the perfect souvenir: you'll always recall your vacation when you see that fabric on your shelf or in your quilts.

8. Finally, don't spend all of your time shopping. After all, the point is to make quilts, not simply to collect fabric.

You'll need to temper these guidelines according to your personal situation. After all, there is no sense buying more fabric than you have space to store or money to pay for. If you can afford it and it gives you pleasure, don't worry about having more fabric than you'll ever use. A fabric collection by itself is every bit as valid as a baseball card collection or a stamp collection. And it's such a creative energizer!

The amount you buy should relate to how much fabric you already have, how much room you have to store it accessibly, how much you can afford, and what use you see for it. My stash is large, while my storage space is dwindling. Lately, I've been buying a yard of most fabrics. If a print looks particularly useful, I'll buy a little more. I'll buy three yards if I think the fabric would make great borders. I'll buy two yards if I think I'll need to waste some fabric to cut it with the print centered just so on the patch.

Your needs may vary. If you are trying to build a collection from scratch, buy one- or two-yard lengths. Otherwise, you'll be using your fabric as fast as you buy it--and that's no way to build a collection!

What a delightful idea: buying fabric just to have it! (Most of us have been doing it for years and feeling guilty about it.) You don't have to feel guilty when you buy more than you need or when you don't use it as planned. You are simply building your stash. It feels wonderful when you put your stash to good use making a beautiful Scrap Quilt, and it's so comforting to know you still have plenty of fabric for the next one!

Father's Day, 60" x 72", original quilt designed and made by Judy Martin, 1989. Sashes appear to weave in and out of the blocks, an effect achieved by combining pieced sashes and an unexpected, scrappy block coloring.

Father's Day quilt segment, 34" x 34". The same block and pieced sashing look completely different in this uncomplicated version in just two fabrics.

Father's Day block photos and diagrams are on pages 66-67. A diagram for the pieced sashing is on page 81. The coloring book block is on page 136. Instructions for both versions of the quilt are on page 144.

Marching Band, 66" x 80", original quilt designed and made by Judy Martin, 1989-1990. Pieced sashes and setting squares expand simple blocks into an overall design. Scraps in a red, white, and blue color scheme add interest.

Marching Band quilt segment, 45" x 45". The same block and set is interpreted in a different color scheme and just a few fabrics. The effect is less busy.

The Marching Band block photos and diagram are on pages 64-65. The pieced sash and setting square are on page 81. The coloring book block is on page 135. Instructions for making both versions of the quilt are on page 145.

Sweethearts' Star, 57" x 75", original quilt designed and made by Judy Martin, 1990. The Sweethearts' Star block and Wedding Band, a simple pieced alternate block, combine to suggest interlocking rings.

Sweethearts' Star quilt segment, 27" x 27". This version is made from just a few fabrics.

Sweethearts' Star block photos and diagram are on pages 62-63. Wedding Band block photos and diagram are on pages 76-77. Coloring book blocks are on pages 135 and 137. Quilt instructions are on page 145.

Picnic in the Park, 71" x 87", original quilt designed and made by Judy Martin, 1989. A multitude of pastel scraps creates a lively, variegated surface. The color scheme shifts from block to block, and individual blocks are apparent despite the secondary, overall pattern of blue chains running through the blocks and pieced sashes.

Picnic in the Park quilt segment, 34" x 34". The same pairing of blocks and pieced sashes looks traditional in a counterchange of a single red print and plain muslin.

Block photos and diagram, pages 64-65; pieced sash, 81; coloring book block, 135; quilt instructions, 146.

FRIENDSHIP QUILTS & SAMPLER QUILTS

Some of the most memorable quilts are Friendship Quilts or Sampler Quilts. Friendship Quilts include blocks or patches signed by many different friends. Sampler Quilts include blocks of many different patterns. Often, a quilt is both a Friendship Quilt and a Sampler Quilt, with blocks of many patterns made and signed by many friends. Friendship Quilts have long been favorites, perhaps because the participation of friends adds meaning to the quilt. Sampler Quilts can have extra meaning, as well. Each block can have special significance, with the block names relating to the maker's personal history.

FRIENDSHIP QUILTS

Friendship Quilts come in many varieties. They can be samplers of many different blocks, or they can include just one or two blocks repeated many times. They can be made from scraps or just a few fabrics. They can be based on a color scheme or include a little bit of every color. What all friendship quilts have in common is the participation of friends and the inclusion of some remembrance from each participant.

The remembrance is most often a signature. Sometimes, a few words, a drawing, or favorite saying are added to the signature patch. Additionally, participants may be asked to make a block or send a scrap of fabric for inclusion in the quilt.

A few traditional quilt blocks were designed specifically for Friendship Quilts, with space for a signature in the center. In the past, Friendship Quilts often were made from ordinary blocks having large center patches. For this book, I have designed dozens of new blocks suitable for signatures. They are shown on pages 98-109.

Initiating a Friendship Quilt project requires a little organization. You will be responsible for more than simply choosing a pattern and a color scheme. You will need to gather materials and instructions and distribute them to your friends. With a little preparation on your part, you can assure the success of your project. Try to anticipate any questions or problems in the planning stage. Here are some guidelines for organizing your Friendship Quilt project.

ORGANIZING A FRIENDSHIP QUILT PROJECT

If your friends will be making blocks or sending fabric, be sure to specify the color scheme. If you are not particular about colors, let your friends know they can use any color they desire.

If you are providing the pattern, keep it simple and accurate.

If you want the colors or values to follow a certain plan, provide a sketch.

If you want the block to go with a certain sashing fabric, provide a swatch.

If you want each block to include a particular fabric, provide ample fabric.

If your friends will be making blocks of their own choice, specify a block size (or tell them it doesn't matter). Be clear about whether or not dimensions include seam allowances.

If you ask for fabric, specify dimensions that are generous enough for you to cut extra patches or to position your pattern(s) on the fabric in the best way to take advantage of print and grain.

Whatever you do, allow more time than it should take (two weeks to a month to sign a signature patch sent by mail; one or two months to make a block).

Make it easy for your friends by offering to come by to pick up nearby friends' finished blocks or patches. For far-away friends, provide a self-addressed envelope large enough to accommodate the block or patch . Be sure to affix sufficient postage for what you expect them to send.

Send thank-you notes when the blocks or patches arrive. The best part of making a Friendship Quilt is getting in touch with all of your friends. A thank-you note is another opportunity to stay in touch. Later, when you have finished making the quilt, send each participant a snapshot of the quilt that they helped make. You can show off a little, and you'll make your friends feel very important.

Once you have begun thinking about your Friendship Quilt project, you will realize that there are many ways to go about it. You will need to plan not only the quilt, but also the nature of your friends' participation. Before deciding what kind of Friendship Quilt to make, you will want to consider your friends' quiltmaking experience. If the participants are all experienced quilters, you can ask each one to make a block. If many are beginners, you can ask for a simple block or for just a piece of fabric that you can cut and stitch into your quilt. If many of your friends don't sew at all, just ask for a signature. Furthermore, you'll need to do some extra planning to insure that the signature patches turn out the way you want them and stay perfect for years to come. Here are some suggestions to consider.

OPTIONS FOR FRIENDSHIP QUILTS

1. Ask each friend to make a block from a pattern that you provide.

2. Ask each friend to make the block of her choice. You may specify a color scheme or size, if desired.

3. Ask each friend to exchange friendship blocks with you. Each of you may specify a theme or colors for your own quilt.

4. Ask less experienced friends to make just part of a block (for example, the octagon and the four triangles in the center of Sugar Bowl on page 78). Make the rest of the block yourself.

5. Ask each friend for a piece of fabric, which you will include in the quilt.

6. Invite your nearby friends to a party-cum-quilting-class, where you will provide the patterns, materials, expertise, and refreshments.

7. Finally, ask each friend for a signature. No matter what you ask for, be sure to get a signature, as well.

GUIDELINES FOR MAKING SIGNATURE PATCHES

If you ask for only a signature, provide the fabric patch and the pen.

Be sure to use a fine-point, permanent marking pen. A Pilot pen with the word "SC-UF" on the barrel is tried and true. If you can't find one of these, test your pen by writing on a scrap of fabric and then washing the scrap. Sometimes pressing the patch after writing on it helps to set the ink.

Prewash the fabric. Press it while damp or spritz it with clear water as you press to get out every last wrinkle. Do not use spray starch, as it may affect the ink.

Cut out the patches. Press a similar-sized piece of freezer paper to the back of the patch to stabilize it and make it easier to write on. You don't have to cut the freezer paper very precisely--you can simply tear it off using the cutter on the box. If you like, you can cut the freezer paper precisely the finished size of the block and center it on the patch to indicate the maximum writing area. If desired, you can rule a line on the freezer paper (it will show through the fabric if the patch is held up to a sunny window) to help keep signatures straight. Be sure to tell your friends to sign on the fabric side of the patch, not on the freezer paper.

If you are particular about having the signature centered on the patch, cut the patch two or three inches longer and wider than the finished patch measurements. This way, you can make adjustments for friends who miscalculate. Cut the freezer paper the smaller size of the actual patch to indicate the maximum writing area. After the patch is signed, cut it down to size, centering the signature.

If any of the following makes some difference to you, be sure to advise your friends: Indicate whether you want first names only or first and last names. Let your friends know if they can print their names or if you prefer cursive writing. Indicate approximately how large you want them to write and whether you want just a name or a name plus a favorite saying or a personal comment.

Before sewing, press each signed patch to set the ink, and while it is still warm, peel off the freezer-paper backing.

Kate's Friendship Sampler, 69" x 93", original quilt designed and made by Judy Martin, 1990. Each block is a different pattern incorporating a signature patch and two squares that complete a muslin cross in the block center. A variety of scraps in blue, rose, green, yellow, lavender, and white or cream were used. Patches were signed by my daughter's friends before I made the blocks. Parents signed for children too young to write.

All 24 blocks from this quilt are on pages 98-99 and 102-109. Additional signature blocks suitable for this quilt are on pages 100-101. Coloring book blocks are on pages 136 and 139-141. Quilt instructions, page 146.

Photo Album

Pen Pals

Bits & Pieces

Sewing Basket

Family & Friends

Family Album

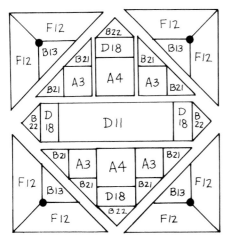

Photo Album, E51, 10", pg. 138

Ask each quilting friend to make just the square block center. You can add the set-in corners.

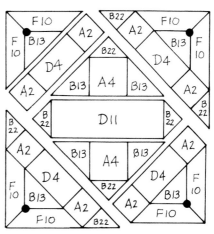

Pen Pals, E57, 10", pg. 138

Mail a muslin patch and a permanent pen to each friend for signing. Join blocks in a pretty Scrap Quilt.

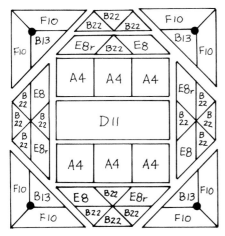

Bits & Pieces, E62, 10", pg. 138

Make blocks from a variety of colors and prints. Then let each friend choose a favorite to sign.

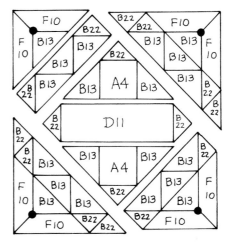

Sewing Basket, E68, 10", pg. 139

This block makes a pretty Friendship Quilt, but the set-in patches are not for beginners.

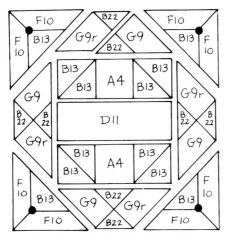

Family & Friends, E57, 10", pg. 139

For a lovely quilt, ask for signatures and fabrics, but plan to stitch the blocks yourself.

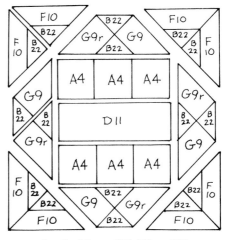

Family Album, C57, 10", pg. 139

Collect striped fabrics from friends. Stitch into blocks with signatures. B, F, and G look great in stripes.

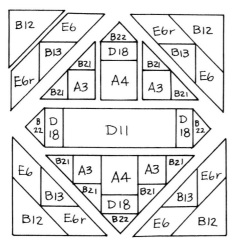

Family Portrait, C57, 10", pg. 139

This block is related to Photo Album and Fraternity Block, but it is easier to make.

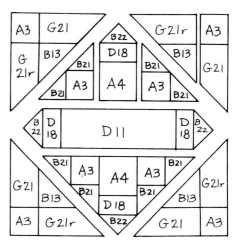

Ice Cream Social, C57, 10", pg. 139

The center is like that of the Photo Album block. The A and D patches must contrast with the signature patch.

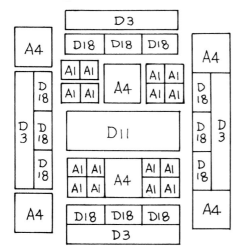

Neighborhood Quilt, A57, 10", pg. 139

Gather friends and neighbors for a quilting bee to make this quilt. A raffle could finance civic improvements.

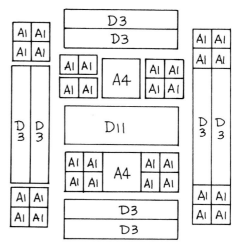

Good Friends, A62, 10", pg. 139

Take the time to write personal notes to friends who participate. Make friendship central to the project.

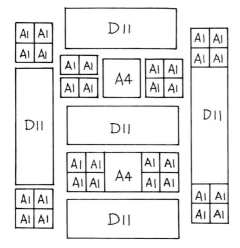

Autograph Hound, A57, 10", pg. 139

Collect signatures on muslin backed with freezer paper. Be sure to send a pen and a return envelope.

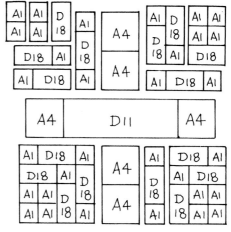

Teamwork, A80, 10", pg. 139

Take a pen and patches to a game to gather teammates' signatures for a quilt you will cherish forever.

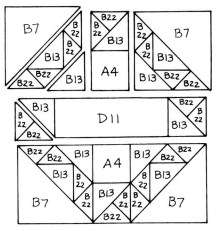

Home Town, C62, 10", pg. 139

Next time you visit your home town, buy fabrics for this quilt and ask old friends for signatures.

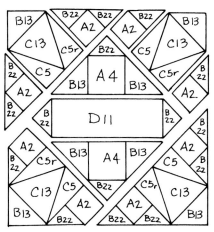

Friends & Neighbors, C68, 10", pg. 139

An easy and enjoyable way to gather signatures is to invite everyone to a party for signing patches.

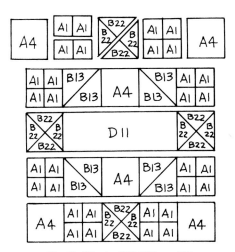

Family Picnic, C91, 10", pg. 139

When your whole clan gets together, get everyone's signature. Show off your quilt at the next gathering.

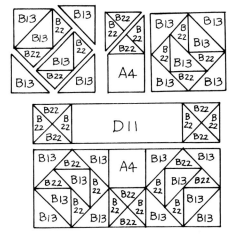

Class Reunion, C86, 10", pg. 139

Go to your class reunion armed with patches and pens to get signatures and comments to include in this quilt.

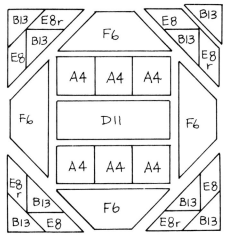

Heartfelt, C39, 10", pg. 139

The block center is easy enough for anyone to master. Consider finishing the blocks for beginners.

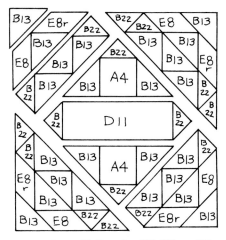

John Hancock's Favorite, C74, 10", pg. 139

This block makes a suitably elegant frame for a prized autograph; made into a quilt, it showcases a collection.

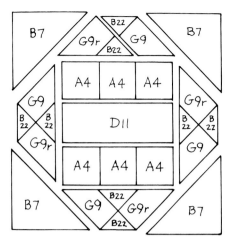

Best of Friends, C39, 10", pg. 140

Most quilters should have no trouble with this block. Ask beginners to make just the center (6 A's and 1D).

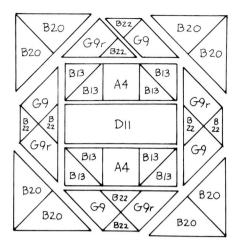

My Old School, C51, 10", pg. 140

A striped fabric adds a special touch to the background. This is a good block for intermediate-level quilters.

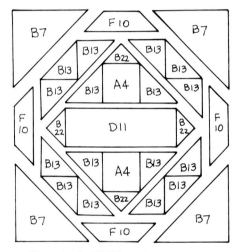

Home for the Holidays, C45, 10", pg. 140

Take care not to stretch the bias edges when you make this block. Press seams away from the center.

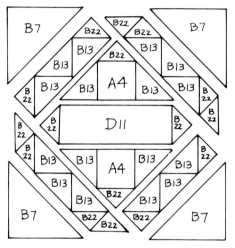

Back to School, C57, 10", pg. 140

Gather signatures from school chums, past or present, and stitch into a quilt full of memories.

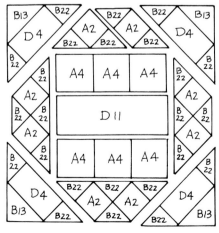

Quilting Bee, C68, 10", pg. 140

This is an intermediate-level block, suitable for your quilting friends to make. Specify a color scheme.

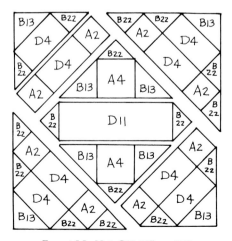

Forget-Me-Not, C62, 10", pg. 140

Ask each friend for fabric to cut the B13's. The variety of colors and fabrics will provide a good accent.

Best of Friends

My Old School

Home for the Holidays

Back to School

Quilting Bee

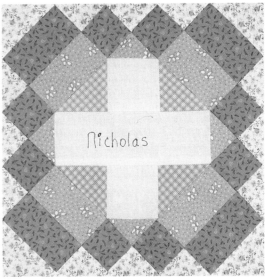

Forget-Me-Not

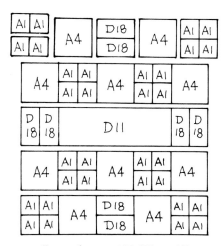

Remembrance, A74, 10", pg. 140

*Set blocks with 3" sashes and 9-patch setting squares.
In each block, use a different pink print for the chains.*

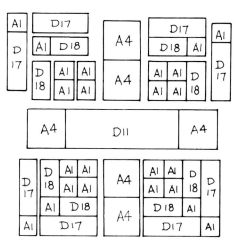

Sentimental Journey, A68, 10", pg. 140

*This is a good block for teaching patchwork to friends.
Have a Friendship Quilt party to share the fun.*

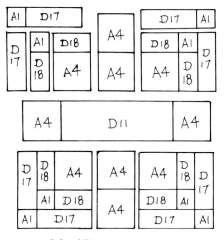

School Days, A51, 10", pg. 140

*Set blocks with 3" sashes and 9-patch setting squares.
Your friends should enjoy making this block.*

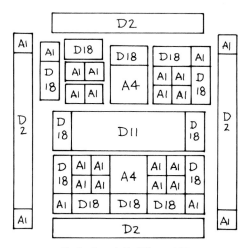

Yesterday, A62, 10", pg. 140

*This block is easy enough to ask friends to make. Ask
beginners for the block center; make the rest yourself.*

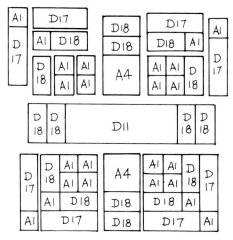

Scrapbook, A74, 10", pg. 140

*This easy block is an excellent choice to ask friends to
make. Provide muslin for the B and D patches.*

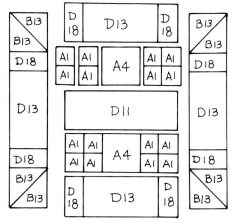

Homecoming, B57, 10", pg. 140

*Frame each block with B and D patches cut from a
different striped fabric. The sewing in this is easy.*

Remembrance

Sentimental Journey

School Days

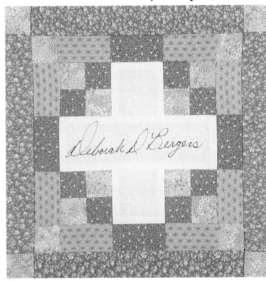

Yesterday

Scrapbook

Homecoming

Family Reunion

Fireworks

Home Team

Anniversary Block

Classmates

Fraternity Block

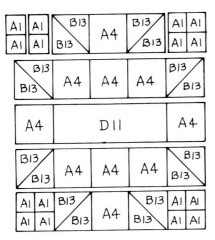

Family Reunion, B62, 10", pg. 136

This is a simple block for friends with quiltmaking experience. Ask for scrap blocks in specified colors.

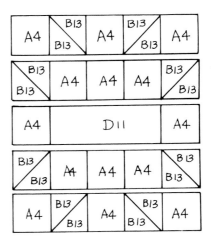

Fireworks, B45, 10", pg. 136

Its ease of construction makes this block ideal for a Friendship Quilt block exchange.

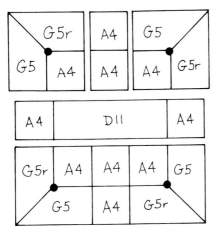

Home Team, E28, 10", pg. 140

The center of this block is exceptionally easy. Add the corners, with the set-in patches, yourself.

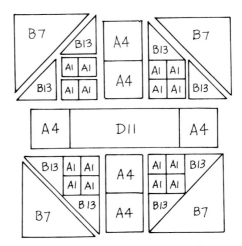

Anniversary Block, B51, 10", pg. 140

Collect friends' signatures beforehand, and make a quilt to present at a golden anniversary party.

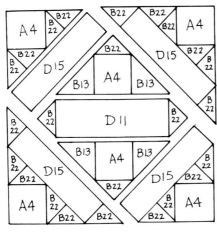

Classmates, C57, 10", pg. 140

Collect autographs from school chums and make a lovely scrap quilt in this pattern to remember them by.

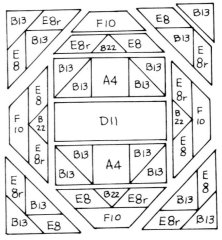

Fraternity Block, C62, 10", pg. 141

Collect signatures from fellow members of a college or civic group. Share a photo of the finished quilt.

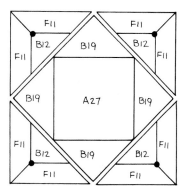

Sorority Block, E17, 12", pg. 141

This block has plenty of space for signatures, drawings, and comments. Plan to add the corners yourself.

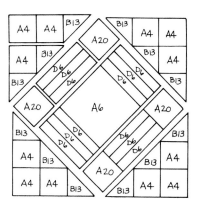

Rotary Block, C41, 12", pg. 141

Press seams toward the rectangles for smooth joints. Be sure to have the signatures done diagonally.

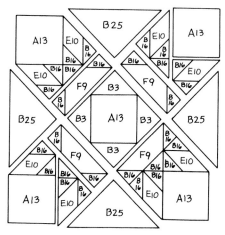

Album Patch, C39, 14", pg. 141

Here is an old-fashioned star to surround a signed square. This would be attractive in patriotic solids.

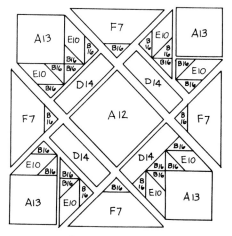

Family Tree, C33, 14", pg. 141

This makes a beautiful quilt. The center square is large enough for a whole branch of the family to sign.

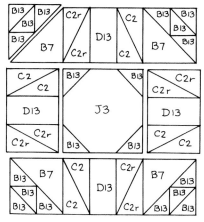

Marine Corps Block, C33, 14", pg. 141

Gather signatures from military buddies to make a quilt that will have special meaning.

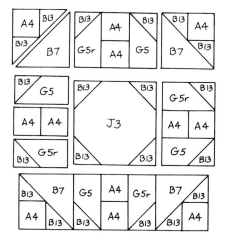

Coast Guard Block, C33, 14", pg. 141

Set this block with 2" or 3" sashes. You can make a large quilt with just 20 or 25 blocks.

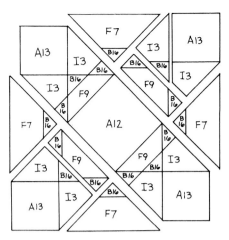

Army Block, C27, 14", pg. 141

Iron on freezer-paper backing to each signature patch. Rule a diagonal to indicate the space for a signature.

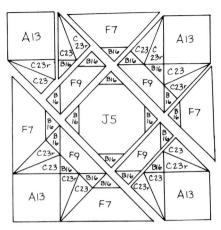

Navy Block, C36, 14", pg. 141

Getting in touch with old friends is half the fun of a Friendship Quilt project. Then be sure to stay in touch.

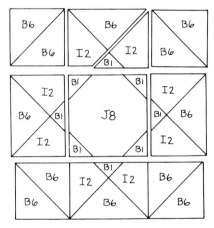

Air Force Block, C21, 14", pg. 141

Be sure to test your pen for permanence before getting signatures. You'll want your quilt to last.

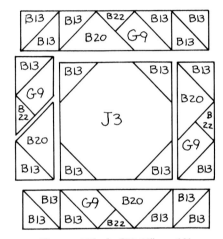

Veterans' Block, C48, 10", pg. 141

Make this quilt as a fund raiser. Get plenty of quilters involved to make quick work of it.

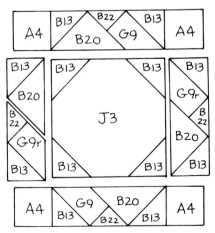

Alma Mater, C42, 10", pg. 141

Cut the G patches in mirror images by folding the fabric and cutting through two or four layers at a time.

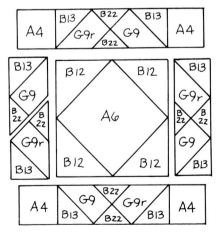

Hometown Hero, C48, 10", pg. 141

This would make a handsome presentation quilt. Signed by friends, it would have lasting meaning, too.

SAMPLER QUILTS

A Sampler Quilt includes many different blocks. Each block may be made by a different person, or one person can make all of the blocks.

Often, beginning quiltmaking classes are developed around a Sampler Quilt project. Each different block is chosen as an example of a new skill. By the time she has completed her Sampler Quilt, the student will have mastered a variety of quiltmaking techniques. In these beginner quilts, all blocks are usually the same size and all are made from the same few fabrics. Blocks are joined in rows with sashing strips. However, this is just one of many ways of putting together a Sampler Quilt.

A Sampler Quilt can be exciting visually. The use of scrap fabrics adds delightful nuances of color and shading. Blocks can be made in a variety of sizes for something out of the ordinary. Blocks can be set in a different arrangement from the usual sashed set. For example, they can be arranged randomly, with no discernable rows.

A Sampler Quilt can also have great personal meaning. Blocks can be chosen for the significance of their names. The personal history of the maker or recipient is told in block names that reflect the experience and interests of that individual. The block, A Long Way to Tipperary, might signify an Irish heritage. The Boston's Best block might represent a home town. The Sewing Basket block might stand for an interest in dressmaking or quilting. A list of block names and their meanings can be stitched to the back of the quilt to convey this special significance for generations to come.

Here are some different ideas for samplers:

IDEAS FOR SAMPLER QUILTS

1. Make blocks of all sizes from scraps of all colors and arrange them haphazardly, filling in with odd patches where necessary. This makes an exciting quilt. The Personal History Sampler Quilt made for *Judy Martin's Ultimate Book of Quilt Block Patterns* and shown here on page 112 was made this way.

2. Make blocks of several sizes and in many colors. Frame the smaller blocks with narrow strips to enlarge them to match the largest blocks in size. Join blocks in rows with sashes cut from scraps or from a single fabric. (Judy's Friendship Sampler, page 112, was made this way.)

3. Select a pleasing array of solid colors from which to make blocks.

4. Choose a color scheme, and make blocks from many scraps in these colors. (The Log Cabin Sampler on the inside front cover was made this way.)

5. Make a sampler of signature blocks. Each block might have the same center motif for continuity. Friends can sign patches for the blocks. (Kate's Friendship Sampler, page 97, was made this way.)

6. Make a scrap sampler using a theme-and-variations idea. One block or several related blocks can be interpreted many ways, with color and fabric placement utilized to highlight differences. The bonus blocks diagrammed but not photographed in the book provide plenty of related patterns for this kind of sampler. (The Rabbit's Foot quilt on page 84 is a model for a theme-and-variations sampler using only one block.)

Family Reunion, 79" x 99", above, original quilt designed and made by Judy Martin, 1990. The Family Reunion block was designed for Kate's Friendship Sampler (page 97). Here, it is interpreted in scraps in a different color scheme and paired with the Sugar Bowl block to create an interesting all-over pattern. Before I made the blocks, signature patches were sent to members of my family to be signed.

Fireworks quilt segment, 30" x 30", right. This is a slight variation of the larger quilt, with the similar Fireworks block substituted for the more complicated Family Reunion block. Fireworks blocks alternate with Sugar Bowl blocks for an all-over pattern. Just a few, patriotic prints are used.

The Family Reunion and Fireworks blocks are on pages 66-67 and 106-107; Sugar Bowl is on page 78-79. Coloring book blocks are on pages 136 and 137. Instructions for making both quilts are on page 147.

Judy's Friendship Sampler, 97" x 97", above. I asked each friend to make and sign a block of her choice incorporating one of the following list of colors: blue, teal, olive, gold, brown, pink, turkey red, and black. The list was long because I wanted a scrappy look. As I had hoped, blocks came in a variety of sizes. I added one-inch strips to the smaller blocks to make all blocks 14". The strong paisley print in the sashes contributes to the busy look that I wanted. All of the block patterns are in *Judy Martin's Ultimate Book of Quilt Block Patterns.* The blocks and their makers are listed in the acknowledgments on page 4.

Personal History Sampler Quilt, 60" x 74", left. Designed and made by Judy Martin for *Judy Martin's Ultimate Book of Quilt Block Patterns;* complete patterns are in that book. Blocks of all sizes and colors are placed casually, almost randomly. Additional shapes fill the odd spaces. Although rows are not readily apparent, the blocks are joined in four vertical strips. Each block was chosen because its name suggested something meaningful to me.

The Log Cabin is probably America's all-time favorite quilt design. It was popular in the middle of the 19th century and it remains tremendously popular today.

The Log Cabin is easy to make: few joints to match, no points, no curves, no bias edges, just simple squares and rectangles. It is a joy to behold: the Log Cabin invariably looks much more complex and interesting than the construction would suggest. It is a perfect vehicle for scraps and the rush of warm feelings they evoke. The Log Cabin makes any quilter feel creative: It can be set together in so many exciting arrangements that before you finish making one you can't wait to get started on another. No wonder the Log Cabin is so popular!

The Log Cabin block is generally half light and half dark, with a stair-stepped division of color running diagonally across the block. In the quilt, blocks are turned so that light touches light or light touches dark in adjacent blocks to form a secondary pattern. The most popular of these arrangements have names: Barn Raising, Sunshine and Shadows, Straight Furrows, Streak of Lightning. You will find quilts in all four of these favorite sets in the photos in this chapter.

You may enjoy experimenting with these and other, original arrangements after you have made all of your Log Cabin blocks. Before you sew the blocks together, simply lay the blocks out on the floor or pin them to a design wall. Try many different arrangements, if you like. Be sure to stand back to judge the effect. If you come up with an arrangement that you'd like to keep on file for a future Log Cabin quilt, snap a photograph before you dismantle the arrangement. If you prefer, you can use a little "Log Cabin shorthand" to quickly sketch the idea: Rather than going to the bother of drawing all the block details, simply use graph paper, with one square for each quilt block. Draw a diagonal line across each square to divide it into two triangles, and shade the halves that represent the dark sides of the blocks.

Besides all of the exciting possibilities for arranging Log Cabin blocks, there is a whole new range of possibilities within the block details. For this book I have designed almost two dozen new Log Cabin blocks. The thing that got me interested in playing with the details of Log Cabin blocks was a letter from a reader, Brenda Groelz. She sent sketches of a few of her original designs. Among them was a sketch of Flower Chain, a Log Cabin variation. (I made up Brenda's block, and you can see it on page 128.) Brenda's block got me thinking about dividing Log Cabin blocks into thirds or fourths instead of halves. I designed the Smoky Mountain Log Cabin (page 121), and I just kept going from there.

Some of my new designs have stars; some have additional color bands; some have elements of Trip Around the World or Double Irish Chain patterns. Many can be mixed and matched for stunning Log Cabin Samplers, such as the one on the inside front cover. Imagine the fun you can have with Log Cabins now! (I almost didn't finish this book because I was having so much fun with the Log Cabins—there was always one more I wanted to make!)

Log Cabin, trad.

Allegheny Log Cabin

Cascade Log Cabin

Blue Ridge Log Cabin

Pocono Log Cabin

Rocky Mountain Log Cabin

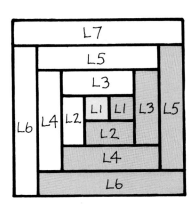

Log Cabin, A30, 7″, 7⅞″, 8¾″

This is the standard, traditional Log Cabin. All of the variations in this book are made in the same fashion.

Allegheny Log Cabin, A49, 9″, 10⅛″, 11¼″

This block was designed to be set next to the Cascade Log Cabin block.

Cascade Log Cabin, C78, 9″, 10⅛″, 11¼″

This block was designed to be set next to Allegheny and Blue Ridge Log Cabin blocks.

Blue Ridge Log Cabin, A74, 9″, 10⅛″, 11¼″

This block was designed to be set next to Cascade and Pocono Log Cabin blocks.

Pocono Log Cabin, A57, 9″, 10⅛″, 11¼″

This block was designed to be set next to Blue Ridge and Rocky Mountain Log Cabin blocks.

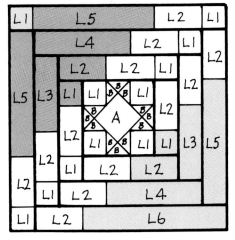

Rocky Mountain Log Cabin, C67, 9″, 10⅛″, 11¼″

This block was designed to be set next to Pocono Log Cabin.

Yellowstone Log Cabin, A57, 9″, 10⅛″, 11¼″

This block is similar to Olympic Log Cabin. Here, though, the bands don't jog but are smooth in all sets.

Glacier Park Log Cabin, A46, 9″, 10⅛″, 11¼″

This block is similar to Smoky Mountain Log Cabin. Here, the bands don't jog when joined in any set.

Black Hills Log Cabin, A45, 9″, 10⅛″, 11¼″

This is similar to Adirondack Log Cabin. Here, the corners permit smooth bands in any set.

Shenandoah Log Cabin, A57, 9″, 10⅛″, 11¼″

This is similar to Cripple Creek Log Cabin. Here the corners complete smooth bands in any set.

Yosemite Log Cabin, A46, 9″, 10⅛″, 11¼″

This is similar to Catskill Log Cabin. Here, though, the corners complete smooth bands in any set.

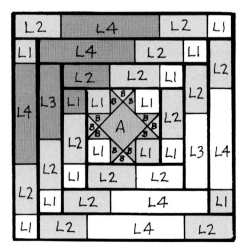

Grand Teton Log Cabin, C71, 9″, 10⅛″, 11¼″

This is similar to Rocky Mountain Log Cabin. Here, the corners complete smooth bands in any set.

LOG CABIN YARDAGE
number of patches that can be cut from 1 yard of 44"-width fabric

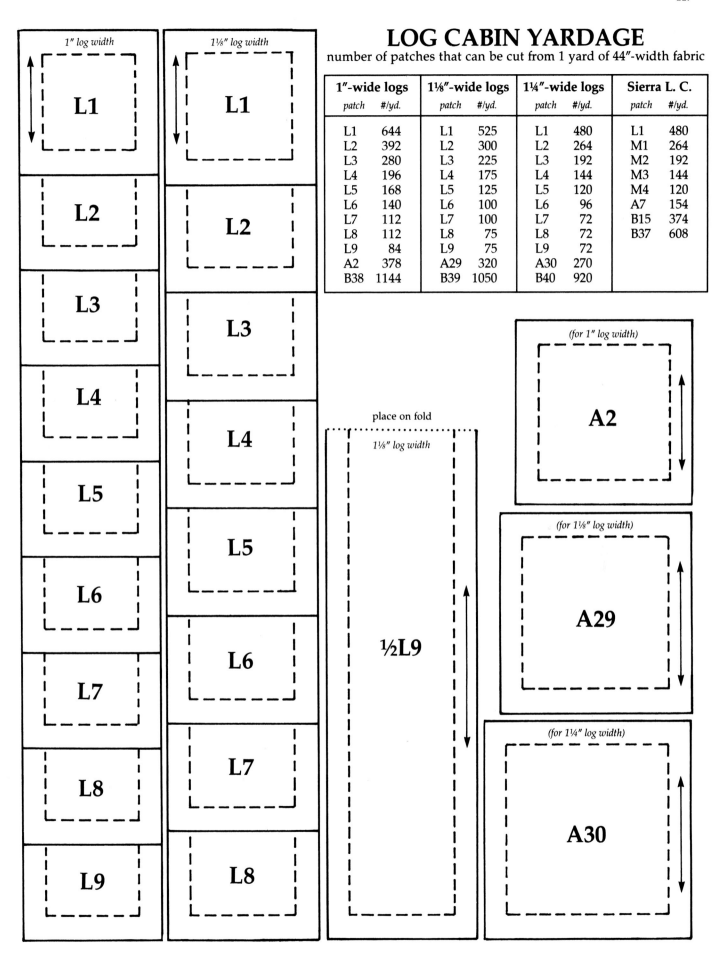

1"-wide logs		1⅛"-wide logs		1¼"-wide logs		Sierra L. C.	
patch	#/yd.	patch	#/yd.	patch	#/yd.	patch	#/yd.
L1	644	L1	525	L1	480	L1	480
L2	392	L2	300	L2	264	M1	264
L3	280	L3	225	L3	192	M2	192
L4	196	L4	175	L4	144	M3	144
L5	168	L5	125	L5	120	M4	120
L6	140	L6	100	L6	96	A7	154
L7	112	L7	100	L7	72	B15	374
L8	112	L8	75	L8	72	B37	608
L9	84	L9	75	L9	72		
A2	378	A29	320	A30	270		
B38	1144	B39	1050	B40	920		

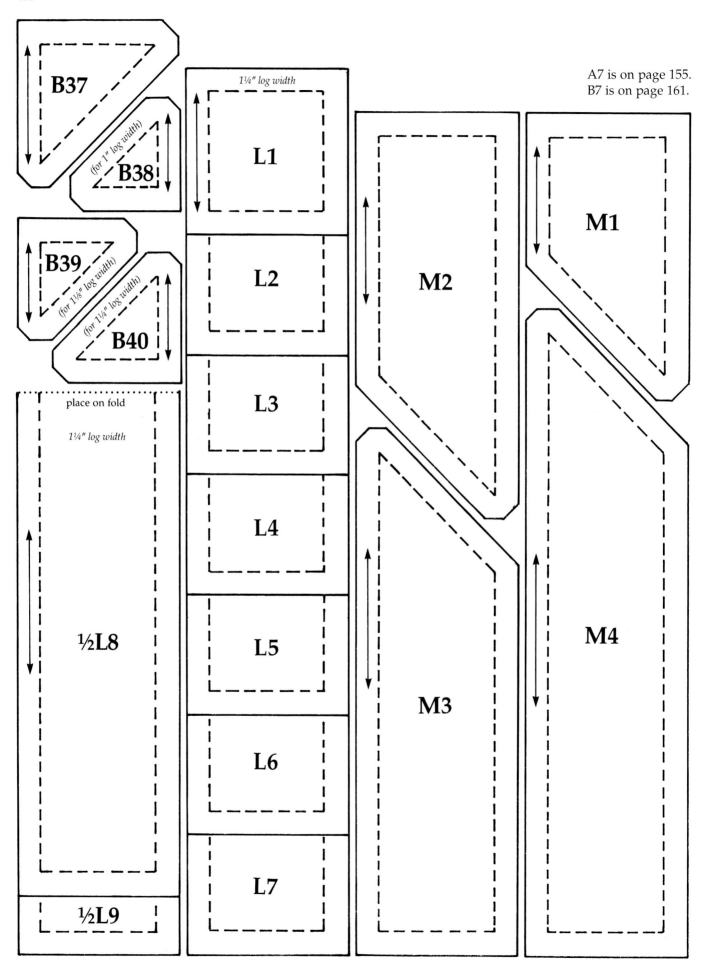

B37

B38 (for 1" log width)

B39

B40 (for 1⅛" log width) (for 1¼" log width)

place on fold

½L8

1¼" log width

½L9

1¼" log width

L1

L2

L3

L4

L5

L6

L7

M2

M3

M1

M4

A7 is on page 155.
B7 is on page 161.

Cripple Creek Log Cabin, 83" x 108", above. Original quilt designed and made by Judy Martin, 1989-1990. This Log Cabin borrows a little from the Double Irish Chain pattern. A double chain of red and orange squares marches down the block. The light logs are interrupted and accented by red logs in the next-to-the-last ring. Blocks are joined in a Sunshine and Shadows arrangement.

Log Cabin, 39" x 39", right. Traditional quilt made by Judy Martin, 1987. This is the basic Log Cabin pattern that quilters have enjoyed for generations. The light and dark block halves permit countless setting variations. This is one of the favorite arrangements, Barn Raising. The block, too, can be varied, as you can see from the other Log Cabins in this book.

Block photos and diagrams for both quilts are on pages 126-127 and 114-115.. Quilt instructions are on page 148.

Weaver's Log Cabin, 59" x 59", right, original quilt designed and made by Judy Martin, 1988. Purple ribbons appear to weave between the logs in this design. Two different Log Cabin blocks alternate to create this effect. Log segments interrupted by the purple ribbons are carefully cut from the same fabric to create the illusion that an individual log is overlapped by the ribbon. Blocks are arranged in a Straight Furrows set. This simple arrangement is ideal for Log Cabin blocks (such as this and the Sierra Log Cabin) that are interrupted by secondary patterns.

Weaver's Log Cabin block photos and diagrams are on pages 126-127. Quilt instructions are on page 149.

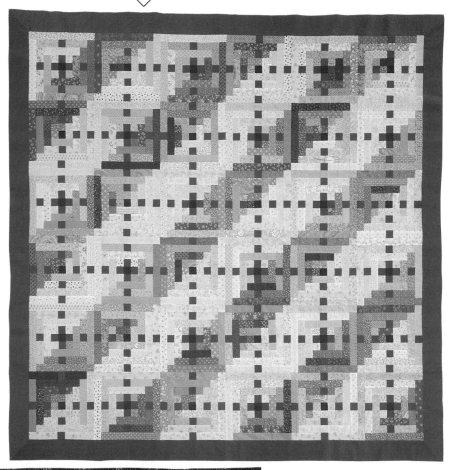

Sierra Log Cabin, 55" x 55", left. Original quilt designed and made by Judy Martin, 1990. Red stars form the block centers and orange triangles radiate out into the rings of logs in this unique block. Lights and darks are carefully selected for uniformity within the half and for contrast between halves of the block. I feel that this is important because otherwise it is easy to lose sight of the Log Cabin in the midst of the stars and radiating triangles. Blocks are arranged in a Streak of Lightning set.

The Sierra Log Cabin block photo and diagram are on pages 126-127. The quilt instructions are on page 149.

Smoky Mountain Log Cabin, 57" x 75", left, original quilt designed and pieced in 1988 by Judy Martin. Each block is divided into three parts: light, medium, and dark. Cornerstone squares in teal and black solids define these areas. Light and dark logs are individual, but medium logs are paired in L's of matching fabric to create a herringbone pattern down the center of each block. Blocks are arranged in a Sunshine and Shadows set. The middle band forms a path between the lights and darks.

Smoky Mountain Log Cabin block photo and diagram are on pages 126-127. Quilt instructions are on page 150.

Appalachian Log Cabin, 36" x 36", right, original quilt designed and made by Judy Martin, 1989. The block combines elements of Log Cabin and Trip Around the World patterns. Blocks are arranged in a Barn Raising set, which echoes the Trip Around the World arrangement. Postage Stamp squares of red, brown, white, and yellow scraps form the Trip half of each block; blue scraps make up the Log Cabin half.

The Appalachian Log Cabin block photo and diagram are on page 128-129. The quilt instructions are on page 150.

Adirondack Log Cabin, 65", x 65", right, original quilt designed and made by Judy Martin, 1990. In this pattern, the block is half light (as usual). The remaining half of the block is divided into medium and dark bands. (Actually, a medium patch is stitched to the end of each dark log.) The division between the two block halves is accentuated by a chain of plum squares. The Adirondack Log Cabin is set in a traditional Sunshine and Shadows arrangement.

The Adirondack Log Cabin block photo and diagram are on pages 128-129. Quilt instructions are on page 151.

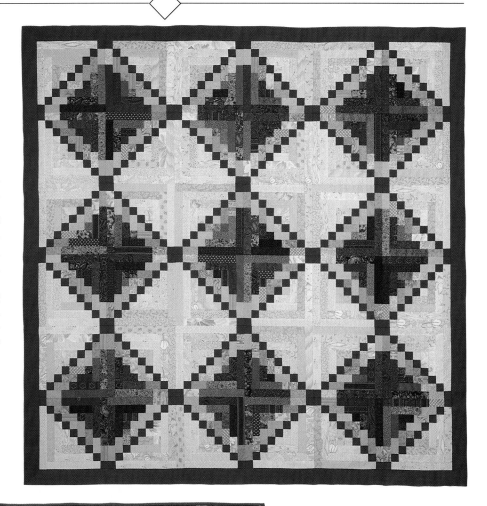

Ozark Log Cabin, 36" x 36", left, original quilt designed and pieced by Judy Martin; quilted by Louise O. Townsend. This quilt was made as part of the 1990 Silver Dollar City Wall Quilt Challenge. Quilts were to be made 36" square and using only certain fabrics and batting from an assortment supplied by the sponsors.

The block here is divided into three parts with a striped panel separating the light from the dark. A star embellishes the block center. The division of the block into three areas instead of two causes an interesting jog in the light and dark paths of the off-center Barn Raising arrangement.

The Ozark Log Cabin block photo and diagram are on pages 126-127. Quilt instructions are on page 151.

USE OF COLOR & SCRAPS IN THE LOG CABIN

Scrap fabrics enrich any Log Cabin quilt. The block is simple and the shapes repetitive, so scraps provide a welcome spark of interest.

Sorting scrap fabrics for a basic Log Cabin quilt is very simple. You can start with a color scheme (such as blue, brown, and white). Select fabrics according to your color scheme and separate them into piles of dark (navy and chocolate in our example) and light (baby blue, tan, and white). If you prefer, you can use many colors rather than a color scheme per se. Simply judge whether each fabric is dark or light.

In a Log Cabin quilt, individual patches need not be clearly defined; contrast between patches is not important. It is the swathes of light and dark that form the overall pattern. Because of this, you can use busy prints, large prints, and multicolored prints with ease. Don't be afraid to use prints having accent colors that fall outside your defined color scheme.

It is easy to use wide ranges of color in a Log Cabin. Rather than just using navy blue and chocolate brown for the darks, throw in some royal blue, teal blue, black, and rust. Instead of just baby blue, tan, and white, add beige, peach and aqua to the lights. Your colors can even clash. A little color tension is always lively.

For some of the Log Cabin variations with medium bands as well as dark and light, you will need to sort your fabrics a little differently. In order for the medium swath to contrast with the light and dark, you will need to keep your lights consistently light, your darks consistently dark, and your mediums consistently medium,. You can shift hues (color) as much as you want, but the range of value (lightness/darkness) should be relatively narrow.

You will also need to plan carefully if your block has star centers. If the stars touch both light and dark logs, as they do in Sierra Log Cabin, page 120, it may be tricky to find a color that contrasts with everything. To make the job easier, you can cut the logs that are adjacent to a darkish star from only the lightest of the lights and the lightest of the darks. For a lightish star, cut these logs from the darkest lights and the darkest darks.

Some designs, such as Weaver's Log Cabin (page 120) and Sierra Log Cabin (page 120), have a secondary pattern that appears to be superimposed on or woven into the Log Cabin pattern. For designs like these with logs that are interrupted by squares, triangles, or other elements, you can enhance the illusion of the secondary pattern by cutting both parts of the interrupted log from the same fabric. If the fabric has a linear design, align both patches on the same part of the print. Where I have cut logs in matching pairs like this, I have indicated it in the cutting chart with a dash between the two patches cut to match.

Sometimes, logs are cut in matching pairs even without these secondary patterns. Rather than individual rectangles of a color, these pairs form L's of one color for a slightly more orderly rhythm. (Cripple Creek Log Cabin, page 119, was done this way.) I usually reserve this coloring for blocks having several rings of logs. Where the logs are short or few, you may find the look is not scrappy enough if you match pairs of logs in L's.

All in all, it is hard to go wrong with color and fabric selection for a Log Cabin quilt in scraps. It is so easy to come up with a glorious combination that you need not hesitate; just jump right in!

LOG CABIN TECHNIQUES

I have treated the Log Cabins a little differently from the other patterns in this book. Let me explain the benefits:

First of all, the full-size pattern pieces for the Log Cabin blocks are presented in this chapter rather than at the back of the book with the other patterns. The reason for this is that I wanted to give you a choice of log widths and block sizes. There are three sets of logs: 1", 1-1/8", and 1-1/4" wide. The corresponding logs from each set have the same pattern letters. This way, you can use the piecing diagram for any log width and block size that you choose. Just be careful to use the same log width to cut all of your patches for a quilt.

Secondly, the block piecing diagrams for the Log Cabins are not exploded to show piecing sequence. Because Log Cabins are made concentrically rather than in rows, an exploded diagram won't tell you much about how to piece the block. Instead, I use heavy lines to indicate the units to be made ahead. These units correspond to the patches in a basic Log Cabin, so all of the blocks end up being made the same way. Here are step-by-step directions for piecing the basic Log Cabin:

To construct a basic Log Cabin block, first sew the shortest log to the center square. Proceeding clockwise, add logs from shortest to longest until the block is complete. (Note that the shortest [square] log is labeled L1 in the diagram. The second shortest log is L2; next is L3; and so on. Except for the shortest and longest logs, there are two logs of each length. Generally, one would be dark and one light. Take care to observe the block shading as well as the log length when you sew logs to the block.)

STEP-BY-STEP DIRECTIONS FOR PIECING THE BASIC LOG CABIN

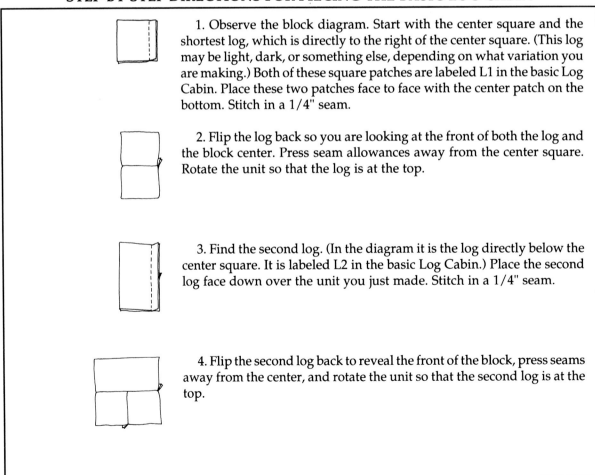

1. Observe the block diagram. Start with the center square and the shortest log, which is directly to the right of the center square. (This log may be light, dark, or something else, depending on what variation you are making.) Both of these square patches are labeled L1 in the basic Log Cabin. Place these two patches face to face with the center patch on the bottom. Stitch in a 1/4" seam.

2. Flip the log back so you are looking at the front of both the log and the block center. Press seam allowances away from the center square. Rotate the unit so that the log is at the top.

3. Find the second log. (In the diagram it is the log directly below the center square. It is labeled L2 in the basic Log Cabin.) Place the second log face down over the unit you just made. Stitch in a 1/4" seam.

4. Flip the second log back to reveal the front of the block, press seams away from the center, and rotate the unit so that the second log is at the top.

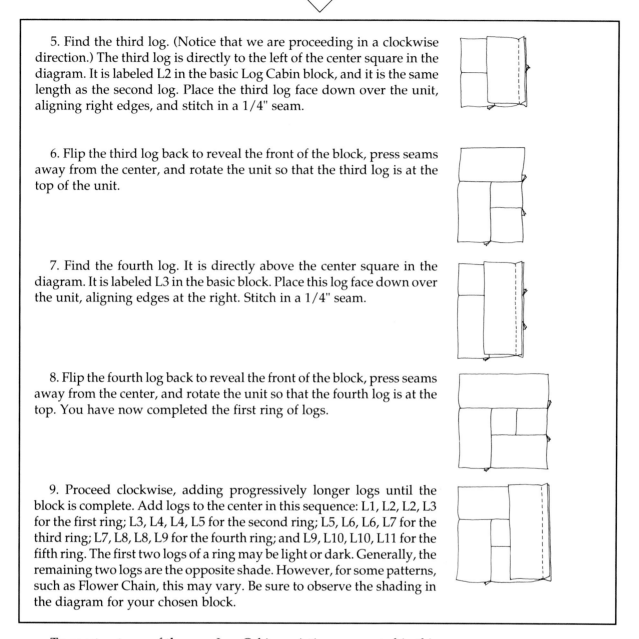

5. Find the third log. (Notice that we are proceeding in a clockwise direction.) The third log is directly to the left of the center square in the diagram. It is labeled L2 in the basic Log Cabin block, and it is the same length as the second log. Place the third log face down over the unit, aligning right edges, and stitch in a 1/4" seam.

6. Flip the third log back to reveal the front of the block, press seams away from the center, and rotate the unit so that the third log is at the top of the unit.

7. Find the fourth log. It is directly above the center square in the diagram. It is labeled L3 in the basic block. Place this log face down over the unit, aligning edges at the right. Stitch in a 1/4" seam.

8. Flip the fourth log back to reveal the front of the block, press seams away from the center, and rotate the unit so that the fourth log is at the top. You have now completed the first ring of logs.

9. Proceed clockwise, adding progressively longer logs until the block is complete. Add logs to the center in this sequence: L1, L2, L2, L3 for the first ring; L3, L4, L4, L5 for the second ring; L5, L6, L6, L7 for the third ring; L7, L8, L8, L9 for the fourth ring; and L9, L10, L10, L11 for the fifth ring. The first two logs of a ring may be light or dark. Generally, the remaining two logs are the opposite shade. However, for some patterns, such as Flower Chain, this may vary. Be sure to observe the shading in the diagram for your chosen block.

To construct any of the new Log Cabin variations presented in this book, the method is similar. First, however, you must join patches to make log units to correspond with the logs in a basic Log Cabin. Each block diagram has heavy lines to indicate these log units. The patches within a unit are simply joined in a row before the log units are joined to make the block.

The block center is also indicated by heavy lines. Some variations have block centers that are larger than the L1 square. For these blocks, join the patches as indicated to make the center square; then make log units. When you assemble the block, you will be starting with log units that correspond with logs in the second ring of the basic Log Cabin.

Quilters who like to use speedy techniques may want to use a rotary cutter to cut strips for logs. This is fine. However, for any of the new variations it is important to cut strips into logs of the proper length before sewing.

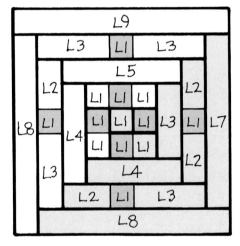

Cripple Creek Log Cabin, A46, 11″, 12⅜″, 13¾″

*For sets other than Sunshine & Shadows, use the
Shenandoah L.C. variation for smooth chains.*

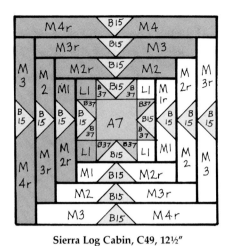

Sierra Log Cabin, C49, 12½″

*Cut M log patches in pairs of matching fabric to be
joined with B15 patches to make rectangular logs.*

Weaver's Log Cabin (1), A41, 9″, 10⅛″, 11¼″

*Cut patches in pairs from matching fabric to make each
assembled log appear to be a single patch.*

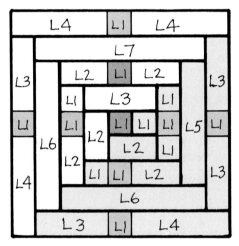

Weaver's Log Cabin (2), A46, 9″, 10⅛″, 11¼″

*Alternate this block with Weaver's Log Cabin (1) in
any set.*

Smoky Mountain Log Cabin, A55, 9″, 10⅛″, 11¼″

*This pattern jogs in Straight Furrows, Barn Raising,
and Streak of Lightning sets.*

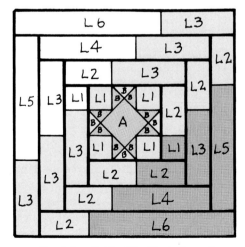

Ozark Log Cabin, C57, 9″, 10⅛″, 11¼″

*A band of striped logs punctuated by a star separates
lights and darks. This pattern jogs in most sets.*

Cripple Creek Log Cabin

Sierra Log Cabin

Weaver's Log Cabin (1)

Weaver's Log Cabin (2)

Smoky Mountain Log Cabin

Ozark Log Cabin

Cumberland Log Cabin

Olympic Log Cabin

Catskill Log Cabin

Adirondack Log Cabin

Appalachian Log Cabin

Flower Chain, designed by Brenda Groelz

Cumberland Log Cabin, A35, 9″, 10⅛″, 11¼″

This pattern makes smooth bands in all sets. Join patches into logs before assembling logs into a block.

Olympic Log Cabin, A41, 9″, 10⅛″, 11¼″

The center band can be one or two medium shades. This pattern jogs in most sets.

Catskill Log Cabin, A41, 9″, 10⅛″, 11¼″

This is similar to the Smoky Mountain L.C., but without the chains of squares separating the bands.

Adirondack Log Cabin, A43, 9″, 10⅛″, 11¼″

Half is light; half is divided into dark and medium bands. This design jogs in most sets.

Appalachian Log Cabin, A46, 8″, 9″, 10″

Half of this block is Trip Around the World rather than Log Cabin. Any set will produce smooth bands.

Flower Chain, A58, 7″, 7⅞″, 8¾″

This block was the inspiration for all of the Log Cabin blocks in this book. It can be colored like a Log Cabin.

QUILT BLOCK COLORING BOOK

This section features ready-to-color line drawings of all of the quilt blocks in this book except the Log Cabins, which quilters don't usually plan on paper, anyway. While the majority of the blocks are also shown in color photographs, it occurred to me that you might want to do a little experimenting with colors of your own choosing. These small block drawings are the perfect size. You can fit enough on a page to see what your quilt will look like, and the small spaces can be colored quickly.

Perhaps you like the color scheme of one block and the pattern of another. By coloring the blank drawing with colored pencils, fine-point felt pens, or crayons, you can combine the elements that you like and see the results before you make the block. Feel free to photocopy the coloring book pages if you want or need to color any block more than once.

You can also use the drawings in this section to help you plan quilts. Photocopy or trace the desired block or blocks and put them together in the set of your choice, with alternate plain blocks or sashes between them or just side by side. Photocopy the assemblage (reducing it, if necessary), and color the quilt drawing, if desired.

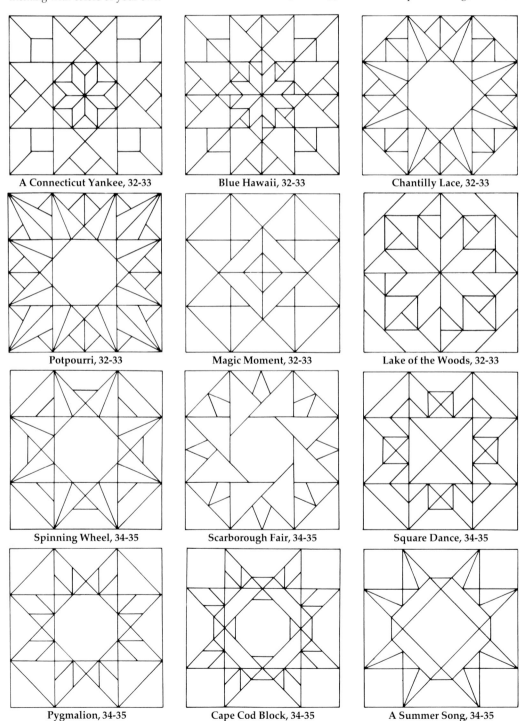

A Connecticut Yankee, 32-33

Blue Hawaii, 32-33

Chantilly Lace, 32-33

Potpourri, 32-33

Magic Moment, 32-33

Lake of the Woods, 32-33

Spinning Wheel, 34-35

Scarborough Fair, 34-35

Square Dance, 34-35

Pygmalion, 34-35

Cape Cod Block, 34-35

A Summer Song, 34-35

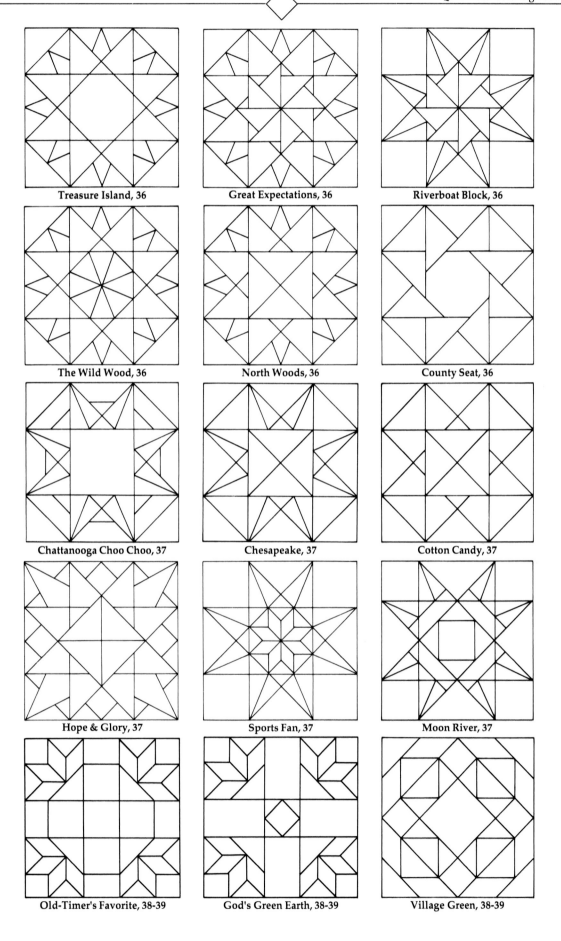

Treasure Island, 36

Great Expectations, 36

Riverboat Block, 36

The Wild Wood, 36

North Woods, 36

County Seat, 36

Chattanooga Choo Choo, 37

Chesapeake, 37

Cotton Candy, 37

Hope & Glory, 37

Sports Fan, 37

Moon River, 37

Old-Timer's Favorite, 38-39

God's Green Earth, 38-39

Village Green, 38-39

Wheel of Fortune, 38-39

Blue Bayou, 38-39

Purple Mountain Majesties, 38-39

Rhapsody in Blue, 40-41

Strawberry Fields, 40-41

American Abroad, 40-41

Wednesday's Child, 40-41

A Summer Place, 40-41

Shropshire Lad, 40-41

The Land of Nod, 42-43

Winchester Cathedral, 42-43

Pins & Needles, 42-43

Heaven & Earth, 42-43

Sunday's Child, 42-43

Camelot, 42-43

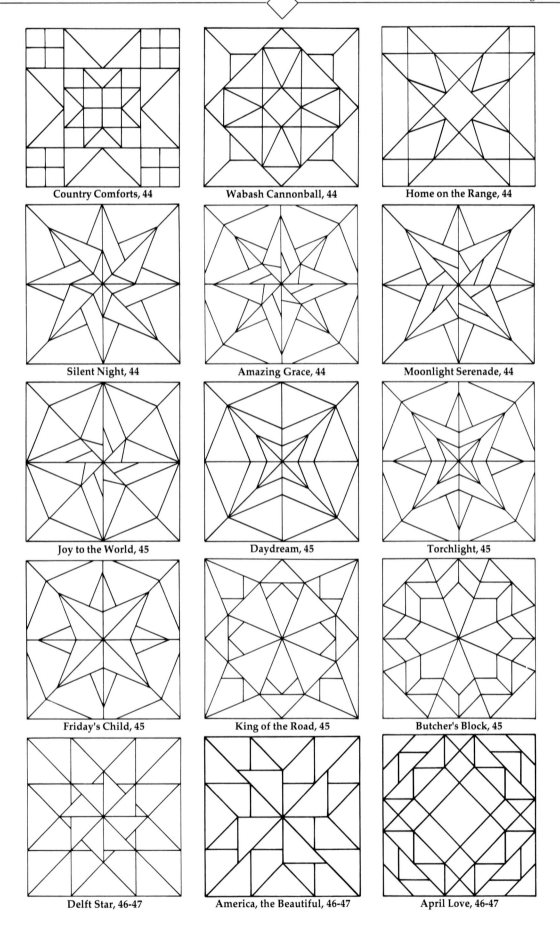

Country Comforts, 44

Wabash Cannonball, 44

Home on the Range, 44

Silent Night, 44

Amazing Grace, 44

Moonlight Serenade, 44

Joy to the World, 45

Daydream, 45

Torchlight, 45

Friday's Child, 45

King of the Road, 45

Butcher's Block, 45

Delft Star, 46-47

America, the Beautiful, 46-47

April Love, 46-47

Wilderness Trail, 46-47

Calico Country, 46-47

Heart of Gold, 46-47

The Wild West, 48-49

Thursday's Child, 48-49

Summertime Blues, 48-49

Field of Dreams, 48-49

Black Beauty, 48-49

Stardust, 48-49

Banker's Hours, 50-51

Charleston Quilt, 50-51

Clothes Line, 50-51

Thunder Bay, 50-51

Dutch Tulips, 50-51

Businessman's Special, 50-51

A Stitch in Time, 54-55

Sea of Tranquillity, 54-55

Boston's Best, 54-55

Twilight Time, 56-57

Sir Lancelot, 56-57

Wonderful World, 56-57

Piecemaker's Block, 58-59, 70-71

Baker Street Puzzle, 58-59

Saturday's Child, 58-59

Quilter's Dream, 62-63

Carnival Ride, 62-63

Sweethearts' Star, 62-63

Marching Band, 64-65

Rabbit's Foot, 64-65

Picnic in the Park, 64-65

Father's Day, 66-67

Family Reunion, 66-67, 106-107

Fireworks, 66-67, 106-107

Pride of Iowa, 68-69

Thorny Crown, 68-69

Colorado Star, 68-69

Green Gables, 70-71

Hudson Bay Block, 70-71

Mother Nature Block, 74-75

Coffee & Danish, 74-75

Around the World in 80 Days, 74

Moondance, 74-75

Heat Wave, 74-75

String of Pearls, 74-75

A Long Way to Tipperary, 76-77

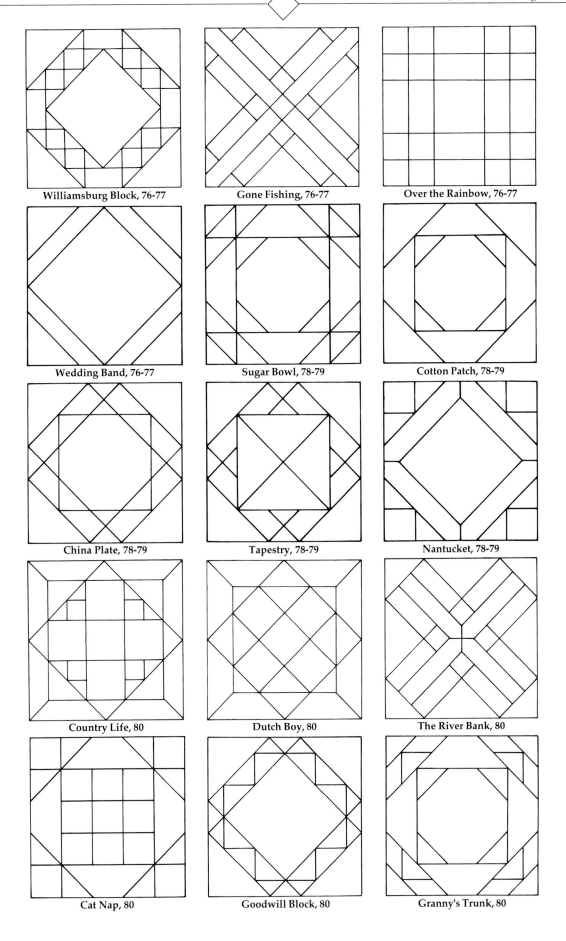

Williamsburg Block, 76-77

Gone Fishing, 76-77

Over the Rainbow, 76-77

Wedding Band, 76-77

Sugar Bowl, 78-79

Cotton Patch, 78-79

China Plate, 78-79

Tapestry, 78-79

Nantucket, 78-79

Country Life, 80

Dutch Boy, 80

The River Bank, 80

Cat Nap, 80

Goodwill Block, 80

Granny's Trunk, 80

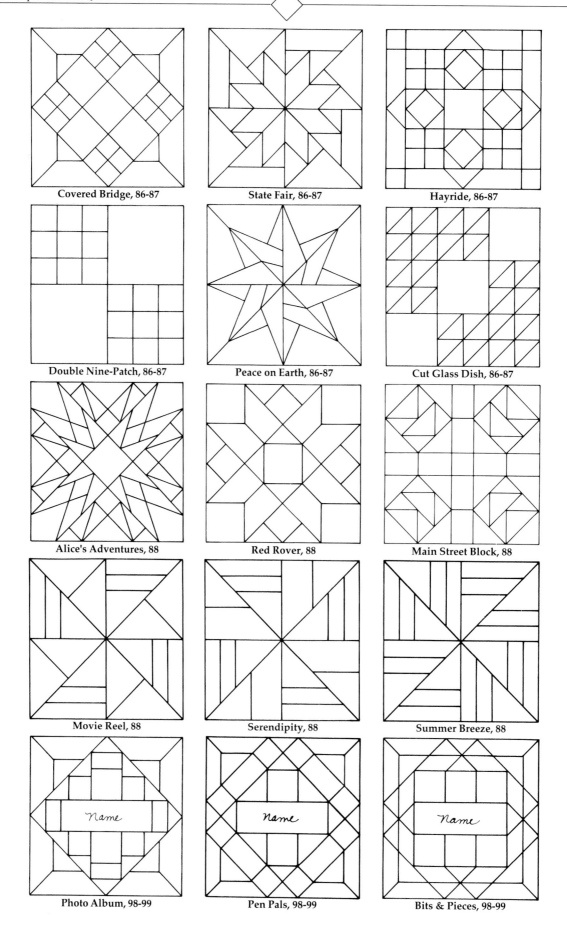

Covered Bridge, 86-87

State Fair, 86-87

Hayride, 86-87

Double Nine-Patch, 86-87

Peace on Earth, 86-87

Cut Glass Dish, 86-87

Alice's Adventures, 88

Red Rover, 88

Main Street Block, 88

Movie Reel, 88

Serendipity, 88

Summer Breeze, 88

Photo Album, 98-99

Pen Pals, 98-99

Bits & Pieces, 98-99

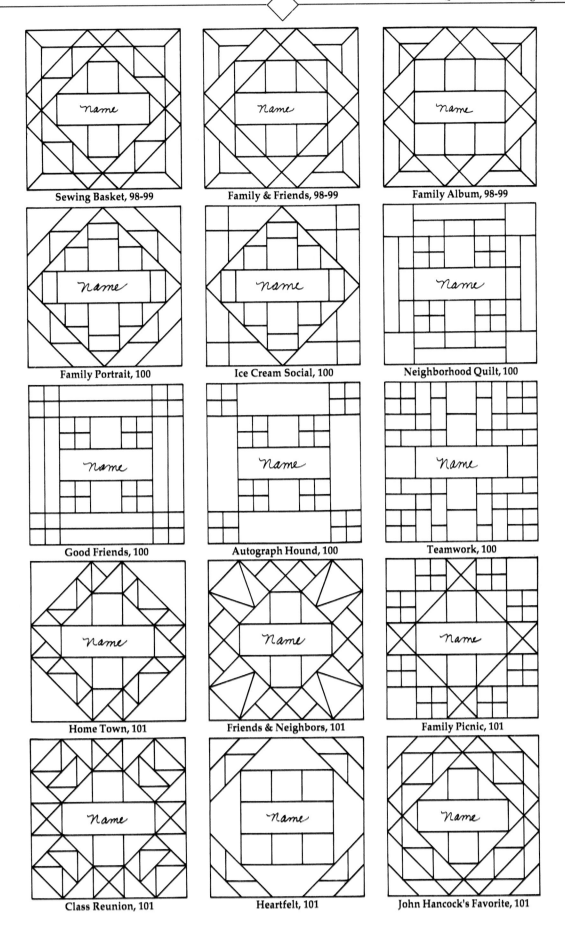

Sewing Basket, 98-99   Family & Friends, 98-99   Family Album, 98-99

Family Portrait, 100   Ice Cream Social, 100   Neighborhood Quilt, 100

Good Friends, 100   Autograph Hound, 100   Teamwork, 100

Home Town, 101   Friends & Neighbors, 101   Family Picnic, 101

Class Reunion, 101   Heartfelt, 101   John Hancock's Favorite, 101

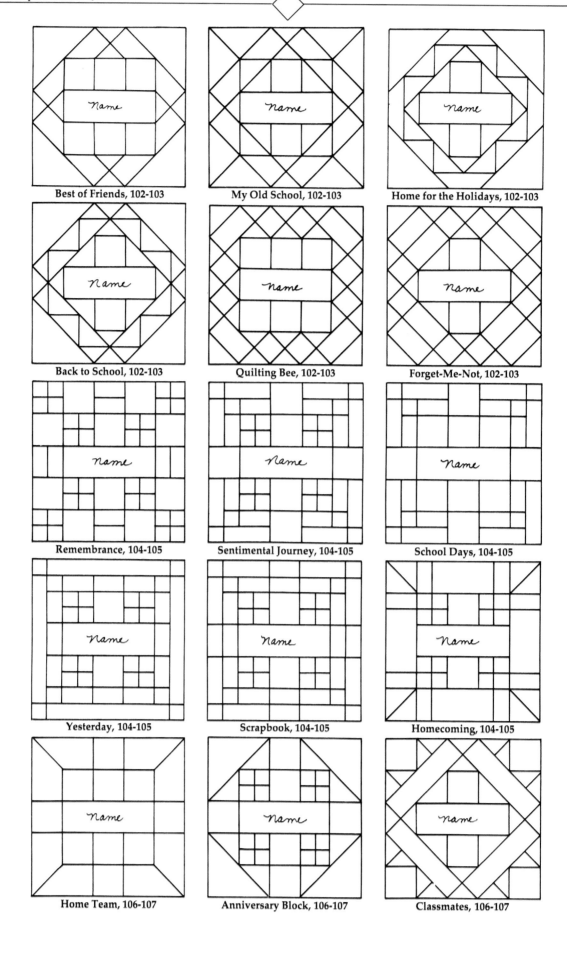

Best of Friends, 102-103

My Old School, 102-103

Home for the Holidays, 102-103

Back to School, 102-103

Quilting Bee, 102-103

Forget-Me-Not, 102-103

Remembrance, 104-105

Sentimental Journey, 104-105

School Days, 104-105

Yesterday, 104-105

Scrapbook, 104-105

Homecoming, 104-105

Home Team, 106-107

Anniversary Block, 106-107

Classmates, 106-107

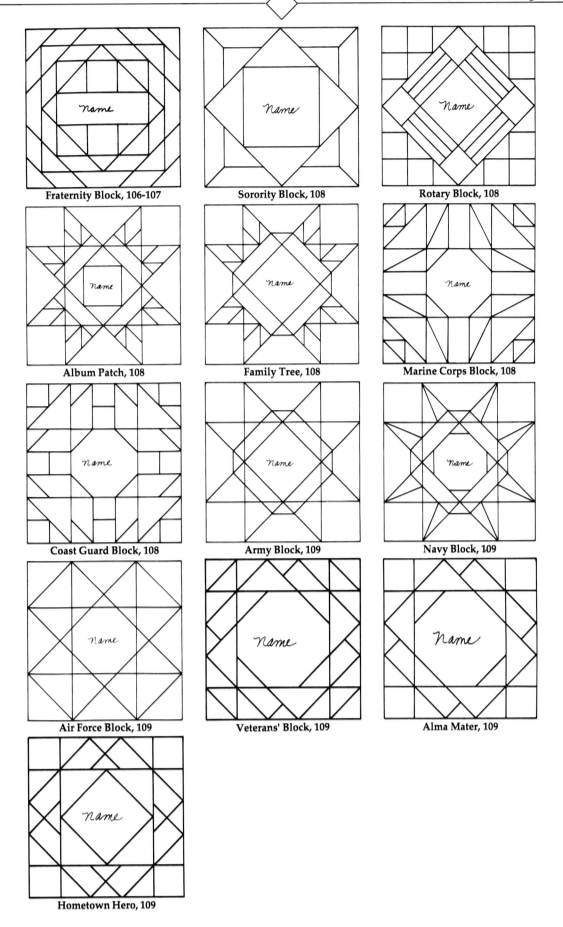

Fraternity Block, 106-107

Sorority Block, 108

Rotary Block, 108

Album Patch, 108

Family Tree, 108

Marine Corps Block, 108

Coast Guard Block, 108

Army Block, 109

Navy Block, 109

Air Force Block, 109

Veterans' Block, 109

Alma Mater, 109

Hometown Hero, 109

QUILT YARDAGES & INSTRUCTIONS

Of course, you can easily make any of the blocks in this book into a quilt. The large, color photograph will guide you in fabric and color placement. The piecing diagram will clearly show how to sew the patches together. The brief description will indicate helpful suggestions. And the charts on pages 28-30 will help you plan an appropriate setting and quilt size and determine the yardage needed to make your quilt.

I have made things even easier for you if you want to make any of the whole quilts shown in the book. For each of these quilts you will find:

1. A chart indicating yardage and cutting requirements for the quilt as shown. (Where there are multiple versions of a quilt, this chart is for the large version.)
2. Helpful hints for making the quilt.
3. Page references for block photos, piecing diagrams, and quilt photos.
4. Full-size pattern pieces (on pages 154-192 for most quilts; on pages 117-118 for Log Cabin quilts).

Beginners needing additional help with a specific technique or with understanding how to join blocks into a quilt should reread the Tried-and-True Quiltmaking Methods chapter and the From Blocks to Quilts chapter.

If you prefer to alter the quilt size or model your quilt after the small quilt segment shown rather than the large version, you will appreciate these helpful charts given with each pattern:

1. A chart listing cutting requirements for a single block/sash/alternate block in the main version. This allows you to easily figure any changes you care to make in the quilt size, setting, or coloring.
2. A chart showing numbers of blocks/sashes/setting squares needed to make the quilt in a variety of popular sizes. This eliminates tedious counting when you plan to alter the quilt size.
3. A chart showing cutting requirements for a single block in the second version where there are two colorings. This is practically another pattern!

To figure cutting requirements for your whole quilt when it is a different size or coloring from the main version, simply multiply the requirements for a single block/sash/setting square/alternate block by the number of each needed for your quilt plan. For example, If you plan to make Rabbit's Foot in the blue/red/tan version in a twin-bed size, see the charts on page 143. The 79" x 96" size listed in the suggested quilt sizes chart would be appropriate. For this size, you will need 20 blocks, 30 setting squares, and 49 sashes, as indicated in the size chart. Now look at the cutting requirements chart for the second version. From red plaid, you will need 5 A4 patches for each block. Multiply 20 blocks times 5 patches per block. The result is 100 patches. You will also need 1 A4 patch for each setting square. The size chart indicates that you need 30 setting squares altogether. The 30 setting squares times 1 patch per setting square equals 30 patches. From red plaid, you will need to cut 100 A4 patches for the blocks and 30 for the setting squares, for a total of 130 altogether. Repeat for each patch. Look up the yardage for each patch in each color in the yardage chart on page 28.

QUILTER'S DREAM

SUGGESTED QUILT SIZES

block size	# blocks	set	# set. sq.	# sashes	border width	quilt size
12″	20	4x5	30	49	1,5,2	74x88
12″	9	3x3	16	24	3	50x50
12″	12	3x4	20	31	4	52x66
12″	36	6x6	49	84	6	98x98

Quilter's Dream quilt photos are on page 83. Blocks are on pages 62-63 and 76-77 (Over the Rainbow); pieced sash and setting square are on page 81. Coloring book blocks are on pages 135 and 137.

CUTTING REQUIREMENTS/YDG.

fabric	per block qty./patch	per set. sq. qty./patch	per sash qty./patch	per quilt qty./patch	ydg.
White Prt.	4 A4			80 A4	1⅝
	4 H8			80 H8	
Pink Prt.		1 A4		30 A4	¼
Pink Stripe			2 D13	98 D13	1
Blue Prt.			1 D13	49 D13	⅝
Blue Scraps	8 A4			160 A4	⅞
Red Scraps	8 B13			160 B13	⅝
Pink Scraps	1 A19			20 A19	½
Green Scraps	4 A4			80 A4	½

VERSION 2

SUGGESTED QUILT SIZES

block size	total blocks	set	# blocks	# alt. blocks	border width	quilt size
12″	9	3x3	4	5	4	44x44
12″	15	3x5	7	8	4	44x68
12″	35	5x7	17	18	4	68x92
12″	49	7x7	24	25	4	92x92

CUTTING REQUIREMENTS

fabric	per block qty./patch	per alt. block qty./patch
Lilac Solid		8 A4
		1 A19
Blue Solid	4 A4	8 A4
		4 D13
Aqua Solid	8 A4	4 D13
White Prt.	4 A4	
	4 H8	
Med. Blue Prt.	8 B13	
Lt. Blue Prt.	1 A19	

RABBIT'S FOOT

SUGGESTED QUILT SIZES

block size	# blocks	set	# set. sq.	# sashes	border width	quilt size
14″	25	5x5	36	60	4.5	97x97
14″	20	4x5	30	49	4	79x96
14″	12	3x4	20	31	4	62x79
14″	9	3x3	16	24	4	62x62

Rabbit's Foot quilt photos are on page 84. The block photo and diagram are on pages 64-65. The coloring book block is on page 135.

CUTTING REQUIREMENTS/YDG.

fabric	per block qty./patch	per set. sq. qty./patch	per sash qty./patch	per quilt qty./patch	ydg.
Blue Plaid			1 K17	60 K17	2⅛
Cream Prt.		1 A14		36 A14	⅜
Var. Scraps	9 A4			225 A4	6½
	16 B13			400 B13	
	4 B7			100 B7	
	4 D13			100 D13	
	4 F15			100 F15	

1. Decide on a size, referring to the chart above.

2. Make the indicated number of blocks, and cut the necessary sashes and setting squares.

3. Join blocks and sashes to make rows. Join sashes and setting squares to make rows. Join block rows and sash rows, alternating types.

4. Add borders, mitering corners.

5. Quilt and bind to finish.

Suggestion: Try varying fabrics from block to block. Vary the placement of values, as well.

VERSION 2

CUTTING REQUIREMENTS

fabric	per block qty./patch	per set. sq. qty./patch	per sash qty./patch
Red Plaid	5 A4	1 A4	
Stripe	8 B13		
	4 D13		
Teal Print	4 A4		
Navy Print	4 B7		
	8 B13		
Cream Solid	4 F15		
Tan Print			1 K17

CARNIVAL RIDE

SUGGESTED QUILT SIZES

block size	# blocks	set	# set. sq.	# sashes	border width	quilt size
12″	20	4x5	30	49	3½	65x79
12″	9	3x3	16	24	3	50x50
12″	30	5x6	42	71	3	78x92
12″	36	6x6	49	84	3	92x92

Carnival Ride quilt photos are on page 85. The block photos and diagram are on pages 62-63. The coloring book block is on page 135.

CUTTING REQUIREMENTS/YDG.

fabric	per block qty./patch	per set. sq. qty./patch	per sash qty./patch	per quilt qty./patch	ydg.
Pink Solid			1 K10	49 K10	1½
Turquoise		1 A4		30 A4	¼
Muslin	4 J9			80 J9	3
	4 J9r			80 J9r	
Scrap Prints	8 C14			160 C14	2
Scrap Solids	8 C9r			160 C9r	1

1. Decide on a size, referring to the chart above.
2. Make the appropriate number of blocks.
3. Join blocks and sashes to make rows. Join sashes and setting squares to make rows. Join rows, alternating types.
4. Add borders. Quilt and bind to finish.

Suggestion: Pair a print patch with a solid patch in a coordinating, slightly darker color.

VERSION 2

CUTTING REQUIREMENTS

fabric	per block qty./patch	per set. sq. qty./patch	per sash qty./patch
Green Stripe	4 J9		
	4 J9r		
Cream Solid	8 C9r		1 K10
Lg. Print	8 C14		
Peach Print		1 A4	

FATHER'S DAY

SUGGESTED QUILT SIZES

block size	# blocks	set	# set. sq.	# sashes	border width	quilt size
10″	20	4x5	12	31	2½,4½	60x72
10″	35	5x7	24	58	4	66x90
10″	49	7x7	36	84	4	90x90
10″	9	3x3	4	12	4	42x42

Father's Day quilt photos are on page 91. Block photos and piecing diagram are on pages 66-67. The pieced sash is on page 81. The coloring book block is on page 136.

CUTTING REQUIREMENTS/YDG.

fabric	per block qty./patch	per set. sq. qty./patch	per sash qty./patch	per quilt qty./patch	ydg.
Dk. Brn./Blk.	4 A4	1 A4		92 A4	1¾
	8 B13			160 B13	
	4 D13			80 D13	
Tan/Gold			2 A4	62 A4	⅜
White Scraps	5 A4			100 A4	1⅛
	8 B13			160 B13	
Teal Scraps			1 D11	31 D11	½

1. Decide on a size, referring to the chart above.
2. Make the indicated number of blocks and pieced sashes.
3. Join blocks and sashes to make rows. Join sashes and setting squares to make rows. Join block rows and sash rows, alternating types.
4. Add borders. Quilt and bind to finish.

Suggestion: Make each block from a variety of scraps to obscure the block boundaries in favor of the overall design.

VERSION 2

CUTTING REQUIREMENTS

fabric	per block qty./patch	per set. sq. qty./patch	per sash qty./patch
Blue Solid	8 B13		2 A4
	4 D13		
Cream Solid	9 A4	1 A4	1 D11
	8 B13		

MARCHING BAND

SUGGESTED QUILT SIZES						
block size	# blocks	set	# set. sq.	# sashes	border width	quilt size
9″	20	4x5	30	49	4	66½x80
9″	9	3x3	16	24	3	51x51
9″	30	5x6	42	71	3	78x91½
9″	36	6x6	49	84	3	91½x91½

Marching Band quilt photos are on page 92. The block photos and diagram are on pages 64-65. The pieced sash and setting square are on page 81. The coloring book block is on page 135.

CUTTING REQUIREMENTS/YDG.					
	per block	per set. sq.	per sash	per quilt	
fabric	*qty./ patch*	*qty./ patch*	*qty./ patch*	*qty./ patch*	*ydg.*
Red Prts.	8 A3	5 A3		310 A3	1⅛
	1 A14			20 A14	
White Prts.	8 A3	4 A3		280 A3	2¼
			2 D19	98 D19	
Dk. Blue Prts.			1 D19	49 D19	⅞
Lt. Blue Prts.	4 A14			80 A14	¾

1. Decide on a size, referring to the chart above.
2. Make the appropriate number of blocks, pieced sashes, and setting squares.
3. Join blocks and sashes to make rows. Join sashes and setting squares to make rows. Join block rows and sash rows, alternating types.
4. Add borders. Quilt and bind to finish.

Suggestion: In order to strengthen the overall design, make each block from a variety of scrap prints in red and white. For focus, make all four light blue patches match in a block.

VERSION 2

CUTTING REQUIREMENTS			
	per block	per set. sq.	per sash
fabric	*qty./patch*	*qty./patch*	*qty./patch*
Dark Blue Prt.	8 A3		
	1 A14		
Med. Blue Prt.		5 A3	1 D19
Blue Plaid	4 A14		
Cream Prt.		4 A3	2 D19
Tan Prt.	8 A3		

SWEETHEARTS' STAR

SUGGESTED QUILT SIZES						
block size	total blocks	set	# blocks	# alt. blocks	border width	quilt size
9″	35	5x7	17	18	6¼	57½x75½
9″	9	3x3	4	5	3	33x33
9″	63	7x9	31	32	4½	72x90
9″	81	9x9	40	41	6	93x93

Sweethearts' Star quilt photos are on page 93. The block photos and diagrams are on pages 62-63 and 76-77 (Wedding Band). The coloring book blocks are on pages 135 and 137.

CUTTING REQUIREMENTS/YDG.				
	per block	per alt. block	per quilt	
fabric	*qty./ patch*	*qty./ patch*	*qty./ patch*	*ydg.*
Pink Prt.	4 C25		68 C25	1¼
	4 C25r		68 C25r	—
		4 B12	72 B12	—
Lt. Pink Scraps	4 C26		68 C26	⅝
Cream Scraps	4 B21		68 B21	1¾
	4 I8		68 I8	—
		1 A28	18 A28	—
Black Scraps	1 A20		17 A20	1
	4 C25		68 C25	—
	4 C25r		68 C25r	—
Black Stripe		4 F16	72 F16	¾

1. Decide on a size, referring to the chart above.
2. Make the indicated number of blocks and alternate blocks.
3. Join blocks and alternate blocks to make rows. Join rows.
4. Add borders. Quilt and bind to finish.

VERSION 2

CUTTING REQUIREMENTS		
	per block	per alt. block
fabric	*qty./patch*	*qty./patch*
Peach Prt.	4 C25	4 B12
	4 C25r	
Peach Stripe	4 C26	
Green Prt.	4 B21	
	4 I8	
Green Stripe		4 F16
Plum Prt.	1 A20	
	4 C25	
	4 C25r	
Cream Prt.		1 A28

PICNIC IN THE PARK

SUGGESTED QUILT SIZES

block size	# blocks	set	# set. sq.	# sashes	border width	quilt size
14″	20	4x5	30	49	2½	71x87
14″	4	2x2	9	12	2	38x38
14″	12	3x4	20	31	2	54x70
14″	25	5x5	36	60	6	94x94

Picnic in the Park quilt photos are on page 94. Block photos and diagram are on pages 64-65. The pieced sash is on page 81. The coloring book block is on page 135.

CUTTING REQUIREMENTS/YDG.

fabric	per block qty./patch	per set. sq. qty./patch	per sash qty./patch	per quilt qty./patch	ydg.
Dk. Blue Scraps	8 A4		2 A4	258 A4	1⅜
Pink Print			2 A4	98 A4	⅝
Yellow Print		1 A4		30 A4	¼
Pastel Scraps	4 A4		2 A4	178 A4	1
White Scraps	4 A4		1 A4	129 A4	2
	4 G5			80 G5	—
	4 G5r			80 G5r	—
Various Scraps	9 A4			180 A4	2⅛
	8 B13			160 B13	
	4 D13			80 D13	

1. Decide on a size, referring to the chart above.
2. Make the appropriate number of blocks and sashes.
3. Join blocks and sashes to make rows. Join remaining sashes and setting squares to make rows. Join rows, alternating block rows and sash rows.
4. Add borders. Quilt and bind to finish.

Suggestion: Choose a separate set of fabrics for each block, but use the same pink print in all sashes.

VERSION 2

CUTTING REQUIREMENTS

fabric	per block qty./patch	per set. sq. qty./patch	per sash qty./patch
Red Print	13 A4		4 A4
	8 B13		
	4 D13		
Muslin	12 A4	1 A4	3 A4
	4 G5		
	4 G5r		

KATE'S FRIENDSHIP SAMPLER

SUGGESTED QUILT SIZES

block size	# blocks	set	# set. sq.	# sashes	border width	quilt size
10″	24	4x6	35	58	6½,3	69x93
10″	9	3x3	16	24	3	44x44
10″	35	5x7	48	82	4	70x94
10″	49	7x7	64	112	4	94x94

Kate's Friendship Sampler quilt photo is on page 97. Block photos and diagrams are on pages 98-99 and 102-107. The coloring book blocks are on pages 136 and 138-141.

CUTTING REQUIREMENTS/YDG.

Version (# blocks)	Sash Fabric qty./patch	ydg.	Set. Sq. Fabric qty./patch	ydg.
24	58 K4	1¼	35 A4	¼
9	24 K4	⅝	16 A4	½
35	82 K4	1⅞	48 A4	¼
49	112 K4	2⅛	64 A4	⅜

1. Decide on a size, referring to the chart above.
2. Make the appropriate number of blocks.
3. Join blocks and sashes to make rows. Join remaining sashes and setting squares to make rows. Join rows, alternating block rows and sash rows.
4. Add borders. Quilt and bind to finish.

Suggestion: Yardage is for setting squares and sashes only. Blocks can be made from a wide variety of scraps, as desired. If you are interested in making a larger version, additional signature blocks suitable for this quilt are on pages 100-101.

FAMILY REUNION

SUGGESTED QUILT SIZES

block size	total blocks	set	# blocks	# alt. blocks	border width	quilt size
10″	63	7x9	32	31	1¼,3½	79½x99½
10″	9	3x3	5	4	3	36x36
10″	35	5x7	18	17	3	56x76
10″	81	9x9	41	40	3	96x96

The Family Reunion quilt photo is on page 111. Block photos and piecing diagrams are on pages 66-67 and 78-79 (Sugar Bowl). The coloring book blocks are on pages 136 and 137.

CUTTING REQUIREMENTS/YDG.

fabric	per block qty./patch	per alt. block qty./patch	per quilt qty./patch	ydg.
Cream Solid	8 A1		256 A1	4
	2 A4		64 A4	—
	8 B13		256 B13	—
	1 D11		32 D11	—
		4 B13	124 B13	—
		1 J3	31 J3	—
		4 F6	124 F6	⅝
Tan Stripe				
Dark Scraps	8 A4		256 A4	2½
		12 B13	372 B13	—
Bright Scraps	8 A1		256 A1	½
Wine Print	8 B13	4 B13	380 B13	1¼

1. Decide on a size, referring to the chart above.
2. Make the appropriate number of blocks and alternate blocks.
3. Join blocks and alternate blocks to make rows. Join rows.
4. Add borders. Quilt and bind to finish.

Suggestion: Cut out the rectangular patches, iron on freezer-paper backing, and distribute patches along with a permanent fine-point marking pen to friends for signing. The octagons could provide additional space for autographs or favorite sayings.

FIREWORKS

SUGGESTED QUILT SIZES

block size	total blocks	set	# blocks	# alt. blocks	border width	quilt size
10″	63	7x9	31	32	3	76x96
10″	9	3x3	4	5	3	36x36
10″	35	5x7	17	18	3	56x76
10″	81	9x9	40	41	3	96x96

The Fireworks quilt photo is on page 111. The block photos and diagrams are on pages 66-67 and 78-79 (Sugar Bowl). The coloring book blocks are on pages 136 and 137.

CUTTING REQUIREMENTS/YDG.

fabric	per block qty./patch	per alt. block qty./patch	per quilt qty./patch	ydg.
Dk. Red Prt.	4 A4		124 A4	1⅛
		4 B13	128 B13	—
Lt. Red Plaid	8 B13		248 B13	⅞
Red Stripe		4 F6	128 F6	1⅝
Navy Prt.	4 A4		124 A4	1⅞
		12 B13	384 B13	—
		1 J3	32 J3	1¼
Beige Prt.				
Beige Solid	6 A4		186 A4	2¾
	8 B13	4 B13	376 B13	—
	1 D11		31 D11	—

1. Decide on a size, referring to the chart above.
2. Make the appropriate number of blocks and alternate blocks.
3. Join blocks and alternate blocks to make rows. Join rows.
4. Add borders. Quilt and bind to finish.

Suggestion: The blocks in this quilt are simple enough that you might ask friends to make them. (Beginners could sew just the center rectangle to the six squares. You could complete the blocks yourself.)

CRIPPLE CREEK LOG CABIN

SUGGESTED QUILT SIZES

log width	block size	# blocks	set	border width	quilt size
1⅛	12⅜	48	6x8	4½	83¼x108
1	11	16	4x4	1½	47x47
1⅛	12⅜	24	4x6	2	53½x78¼
1⅛	12⅜	64	8x8	2	103x103

The Cripple Creek quilt photo is on page 119. The block photo and diagram are on pages 126-127.

CUTTING REQUIREMENTS/YDG.

fabric	per block qty./patch	per quilt qty./patch	ydg.
Dk. Red Solid	11 L1	528 L1	1¼
Orange Solid	20 L1	960 L1	2
Red Scraps	1 L6-L7	48 L6-L7	1⅛
Light Scraps	1 L1	48 L1	2⅝
	1 L2-L3	48 L2-L3	
	1 L4-L5	48 L4-L5	
	1 L8-L9	48 L8-L9	
Dark Scraps	1 L1	48 L1	3⅜
	1 L2-L3	48 L2-L3	
	1 L4-L5	48 L4-L5	
	1 L6-L7	48 L6-L7	
	1 L8-L9	48 L8-L9	

1. Decide on colors and fabrics.
2. Decide on a size, referring to the chart above.
3. Make the appropriate number of blocks.
4. Decide on a set, experimenting with the completed blocks.
5. Join blocks to make rows. Join rows.
6. Add borders. Quilt and bind to finish.

Suggestion: Logs are cut and stitched in matching pairs to form L-shapes. Sew an orange square to each light log and an orange and a red square to each dark log before assembling the block.

LOG CABIN

SUGGESTED QUILT SIZES

log width	block size	# blocks	set	border width	quilt size
1¼	8¾	16	4x4	½,1½	39x39
1	7	48	6x8	1½	45x59
1⅛	7⅞	80	8x10	1½	66x81¾
1¼	8¾	100	10x10	1½	90½x90½

The Log Cabin quilt photo is on page 119. The block photo and diagram are on pages 114-115.

CUTTING REQUIREMENTS/YDG.

fabric	per block qty./patch	per quilt qty./patch	ydg.
Yellow Solid	1 L1	16 L1	⅛
Light Scraps	1 L2	16 L2	⅞
	1 L3	16 L3	
	1 L4	16 L4	
	1 L5	16 L5	
	1 L6	16 L6	
	1 L7	16 L7	
Dark Scraps	1 L1	16 L1	¾
	1 L2	16 L2	
	1 L3	16 L3	
	1 L4	16 L4	
	1 L5	16 L5	
	1 L6	16 L6	

1. Decide on colors.
2. Decide on a size, referring to the chart above.
3. Make the appropriate number of blocks.
4. Decide on a set, experimenting with the completed blocks.
5. Join blocks to make rows. Join rows.
6. Add borders. Quilt and bind to finish.

Suggestion: Don't overmatch fabrics. Include plenty of different shades or hues for the darks. For the lights, don't just use fabrics with white or cream backgrounds. Also use pastel shades of the colors in the dark bands.

WEAVER'S LOG CABIN

SUGGESTED QUILT SIZES

log width	block size	set	# blocks	# alt. blocks	border width	quilt size
1	9	6x6	18	18	2½	59x59
1⅛	10⅛	4x4	8	8	1⅛	42¾x42¾
1¼	11¼	6x8	24	24	1¼	70x92½
1⅛	10⅛	10x10	50	50	1⅛	103½x103½

The Weaver's Log Cabin quilt photo is on page 120. The block photos and diagrams are on pages 126-127.

CUTTING REQUIREMENTS/YDG.

fabric	per block qty./patch	per alt. block qty./patch	per quilt qty./patch	ydg.
Purple Solid	8 L1	8 L1	288 L1	⅝
Dk. Purp. Solid	1 L1	1 L1	36 L1	⅛
Light Scraps	1 L1	1 L2	18 ea.	2¾
	1 L1-L1	1 L3	as	
	1 L4	1 L1-L2	listed	
	1 L5	1 L2-L2		
	1 L2-L3	1 L6		
	1 L3-L3	1 L7		
	1 L8	1 L3-L4		
	1 L9	1 L4-L4		
Dark Scraps	1 L1	1 L1	36 L1	2
	1 L3	1 L2	18 ea.	
	1 L4	1 L1-L1	as	
	1 L2-L2	1 L1-L2	listed	
	1 L2-L3	1 L5		
	1 L7	1 L6		
	1 L8	1 L3-L3		
		1 L3-L4		

1. Decide on colors and fabrics.

2. Decide on a size, referring to the chart above.

3. Make the appropriate number of each block.

4. Decide on a set, experimenting with the completed blocks.

5. Join blocks to make rows, alternating types. Join rows.

6. Add borders. Quilt and bind to finish.

Suggestion: Cut some of the logs in matching pairs, as listed in the chart. Cut these pairs end to end along the lengthwise grain so that they will appear to be one continuous log interrupted by the purple "ribbon."

SIERRA LOG CABIN

SUGGESTED QUILT SIZES

log width	block size	# blocks	set	border width	quilt size
1¼	12½	16	4x4	2½	55x55
1¼	12½	24	4x6	2	54x79
1¼	12½	48	6x8	2	79x104
1¼	12½	64	8x8	2	104x104

The Sierra Log Cabin quilt photo is on page 120. The block photo and piecing diagram are on pages 126-127.

CUTTING REQUIREMENTS/YDG.

fabric	per block qty./patch	per quilt qty./patch	ydg.
Red Solid	1 A7	16 A7	½
	8 B37	128 B37	—
Lt. Orange	4 B15	64 B15	¼
Med. Orange	4 B15	64 B15	¼
Dk. Orange	4 B15	64 B15	¼
Light Scraps	1 A24	16 A24	1
	1M1-M1r	16M1-M1r	
	1M1-M2r	16M1-M2r	
	1M2-M2r	16M2-M2r	
	1M2-M3r	16M2-M3r	
	1M3-M3r	16M3-M3r	
Dark Scraps	1 A24	16 A24	1⅜
	1A24-A24	16A24-A24	
	1M1-M2r	16M1-M2r	
	1M2-M2r	16M2-M2r	
	1M2-M3r	16M2-M3r	
	1M3-M3r	16M3-M3r	
	1M3-M4r	16M3-M4r	
	1M4-M4r	16M4-M4r	

1. Decide on colors and fabrics.

2. Decide on a size, referring to the chart above.

3. Make the appropriate number of blocks.

4. Decide on a set, experimenting with the completed blocks.

5. Join blocks to make rows. Join rows.

6. Add borders. Quilt and bind to finish.

Suggestion: The red and orange solids shift colors in even steps. Hand-dyed fabrics in gradually shifting colors are made by Cherrywood Quilts and Fabrics. They are available in packets at your local quilt shop, or they can be ordered from Quilting Books Unlimited, 1158 Prairie, Aurora, IL 60506.

SMOKY MOUNTAIN LOG CABIN

SUGGESTED QUILT SIZES

log width	block size	# blocks	set	border width	quilt size
1	9	48	6x8	1½	57x75
1⅛	10⅛	16	4x4	1½	43½x43½
1¼	11¼	48	6x8	1½	70½x93
1¼	11¼	64	8x8	1½	93x93

The Smoky Mountain Log Cabin quilt photo is on page 121. The block photo and piecing diagram are on pages 126-127.

CUTTING REQUIREMENTS/YDG.

fabric	per block qty./patch	per quilt qty./patch	ydg.
Teal Solid	6 L1	288 L1	½
Black Solid	6 L1	288 L1	½
Dark Scraps	1 L1	48 L1	1
	1 L2	48 L2	
	1 L3	48 L3	
	1 L4	48 L4	
	1 L5	48 L5	
Light Scraps	1 L1	48 L1	1
	1 L2	48 L2	
	1 L3	48 L3	
	1 L4	48 L4	
	1 L5	48 L5	
Med. Scraps	1 L1	48 L1	2⅝
	1 L1-L2	48 L1-L2	
	7 L2-L3	366 L2-L3	

1. Decide on colors and fabrics.
2. Decide on a size, referring to the chart above.
3. Make the appropriate number of blocks.
4. Decide on a set, experimenting with the completed blocks.
5. Join blocks to make rows. Join rows.
6. Add borders. Quilt and bind to finish.

Suggestion: Cut the medium-colored logs in pairs from matching fabric, as indicated in the chart. Before assembling the block, sew a black L1 and a medium L3 to each dark log, and sew a teal L1 and a medium L2 to each light log.

APPALACHIAN LOG CABIN

SUGGESTED QUILT SIZES

log width	block size	# blocks	set	border width	quilt size
1	6	36	6x6	—	36x36
1⅛	6¾	80	8x10	1½	57x70½
1¼	7½	96	8x12	1¾	63½x93½
1¼	7½	144	12x12	1¾	93½x93½

The Appalachian Log Cabin quilt photo is on page 121. The block photo and piecing diagram are on pages 128-129.

CUTTING REQUIREMENTS/YDG.

fabric	per block qty./patch	per quilt qty./patch	ydg.
Red Scraps	6 L1	216 L1	½
Brown Scraps	6 L1	216 L1	½
Yellow Scraps	6 L1	216 L1	½
White Scraps	3 L1	108 L1	¼
Dk. Blue Scraps	1 L1	36 L1	¾
	1 L2	36 L2	
	1 L3	36 L3	
	1 L4	36 L4	
	1 L5	36 L5	

1. Decide on colors and fabrics.
2. Decide on a size, referring to the chart above.
3. Make the appropriate number of blocks.
4. Decide on a set, experimenting with the completed blocks.
5. Join blocks to make rows. Join rows.
6. Add borders. Quilt and bind to finish.

Suggestion: Use scraps for the Postage Stamp squares in the Trip Around the World half of the block, as well as for the logs.

ADIRONDACK LOG CABIN

SUGGESTED QUILT SIZES

log width	block size	# blocks	set	border width	quilt size
1⅛	10⅛	36	6x6	2	64¾x64¾
1¼	11¼	24	4x6	1½	48x70½
1	9	80	8x10	1½	75x93
1⅛	10⅛	100	10x10	1½	104¼x104¼

The Adirondack Log Cabin quilt photo is on page 122. The block photo and piecing diagram are on pages 128-129.

CUTTING REQUIREMENTS/YDG.

fabric	per block qty./patch	per quilt qty./patch	ydg.
Plum Solid	9 L1	324 L1	¾
Light Scraps	1 L1	36 L1	2¼
	1 L2	36 L2	
	1 L3	36 L3	
	1 L4	36 L4	
	1 L5	36 L5	
	1 L6	36 L6	
	1 L7	36 L7	
	1 L8	36 L8	
Dark Scraps	1 L1	36 L1	1⅜
	1 L2	36 L2	
	1 L3	36 L3	
	1 L4	36 L4	
	1 L5	36 L5	
	1 L6	36 L6	
Med. Scraps	1 L1	36 L1	1⅛
	7 L2	252 L2	

1. Decide on colors and fabrics.
2. Decide on a size, referring to the chart above.
3. Make the appropriate number of blocks.
4. Decide on a set, experimenting with the completed blocks.
5. Join blocks to make rows. Join rows.
6. Add borders. Quilt and bind to finish.

Suggestion: Stitch a medium L2 and a plum L1 to the end of each dark log before joining the rest in the usual Log Cabin fashion.

OZARK LOG CABIN

SUGGESTED QUILT SIZES

log width	block size	# blocks	set	border width	quilt size
1	9	16	4x4	—	36x36
1⅛	10⅛	24	4x6	1½	43½x63¾
1¼	11¼	48	6x8	2	71½x94
1¼	11¼	64	8x8	2	94x94

The Ozark Log Cabin quilt photo is on page 122. The block photo and piecing diagram are on pages 126-127.

CUTTING REQUIREMENTS/YDG.

fabric	per block qty./patch	per quilt qty./patch	ydg.
Wine Solid	1 A2	16 A2	¼
	8 B38	128 B38	
Teal Stripe	4 B38	64 B38	1⅛
	4 L1	64 L1	
	6 L2	96 L2	
	6 L3	96 L3	
Cream Solids	1 L1-L2	16 L1-L2	⅝
	1 L3-L4	16 L3-L4	
	1 L5-L6	16 L5-L6	
Dark Scraps	1 L1-L2	16 L1-L2	⅝
	1 L3-L4	16 L3-L4	
	1 L5-L6	16 L5-L6	

1. Decide on colors and fabrics.
2. Decide on a size, referring to the chart above.
3. Make the appropriate number of blocks.
4. Decide on a set, experimenting with the completed blocks.
5. Join blocks to make rows. Join rows.
6. Add borders. Quilt and bind to finish.

Suggestion: Cut the striped patches carefully, all with stripes aligned in the same place on the patches. That way, the block will appear to have a star superimposed on whole logs.

LOG CABIN SAMPLER

SUGGESTED QUILT SIZES

log width	block size	# blocks	set	border width	quilt size
1⅛	10⅛	36	6x6	2½	65¾x65¾
1	9	36	6x6	2	58x58
1¼	11¼	36	6x6	2	71½x71½

The Log Cabin Sampler quilt photo is on the inside front cover. The block photos and diagrams are on pages 114-115.

CUTTING REQUIREMENTS

fabric	qty./patch	per quilt qty./patch	ydg.
Dark Scraps	16 L1 16 L3 32 L5	16 L2 24 L4	⅝
Light Scraps	32 L1 32 L3 32 L5 32 L7	32 L2 32 L4 40 L6	2¼
Pastel Scraps	204 L1 52 L3 4 L5 32 B	96 L2 4 L4 4 L6	1⅜
Bright Scraps	108 L1 64 B	8 A	⅜
Pink Solids	8 A	64 B	¼
Dk. Teal Prt.	108 L1 32 B	4 A	⅜
Med. Teal Prt.	136 L1		⅜
Lt. Teal Prt.	116 L1 16 B	56 L2	⅝
Peach Prt.	96 L1		¼
Orange Prt.	92 L1		¼
Red Prt.	88 L1		¼
Wine Prt.	84 L1		¼

1. Decide on colors and fabrics.

2. Decide on a size, referring to the chart above.

3. Make four Allegheny Log Cabin blocks, eight Cascade Log Cabin blocks, twelve Blue Ridge Log Cabin Blocks, eight Pocono Log Cabin blocks, and four Rocky Mountain Log Cabin blocks.

4. Arrange the blocks with the four Allegheny blocks in the center, surrounded by the Cascade blocks, then the Blue Ridge blocks. Add the Pocono, then the Rocky Mountain blocks, tapering down to the corners.

5. Join blocks to make rows. Join rows.

6. Add borders. Quilt and bind to finish.

BRICKS & BOARDS

The Bricks & Boards quilt photo is on the inside back cover. This quilt is made without blocks, and it measures 53" x 74-1/4".

CUTTING REQUIREMENTS

fabric	per quilt qty./patch	ydg.
Muslin	8 A4 40 D11	⅝
Scraps	88 D3	⅞
Rainbow Solids	176 B13 16 B22	¾
Purple Solid	9-1x62¼ 2-1x43 2-1/72¼ 2-1x53	2⅛
Light Print	2-4x64¼ 2-4x51	1⅞

1. Referring to the diagrams below, make 18 Unit 1's, 20 Unit 2's, 4 Unit 3's, 8 Unit 4's, 18 Unit 5's, 20 Unit 6's, and 4 Unit 7's.

2. Join ten Unit 2's alternately with nine Unit 1's. Sew a Unit 3 to a Unit 4 to make a corner segment. Repeat. Sew a corner segment to each end of the Unit 1-Unit 2 segment to complete a vertical strip. Make two of these vertical strips.

3. Join ten Unit 6's alternately with nine Unit 5's. Sew a Unit 7 to a Unit 4 to make a corner segment. Repeat. Sew a corner segment to each end of the Unit 5-Unit 6 segment to complete a vertical strip. Make two of these vertical strips.

4. Make four strips of the D4 rectangles in rainbow colors, 44 to a strip.

5. Join signature strips, rainbow strips, and the nine purple plain strips as shown in the quilt photo. Measurements listed in the chart are finished measurements. Add one-half inch to the length and width of strips before cutting.

6. Attach borders in this order: shortest purple (top and bottom); long print (sides); short print (top and bottom); longest purple (sides); medium purple (top and bottom). Quilt and bind to finish.

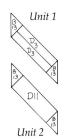

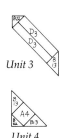

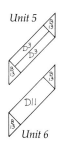

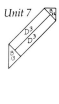

This section includes full-size patterns for all of the blocks and quilts in the book, except the Log Cabins, patterns for which are on pages 117-118. Each patch has seam lines (dashed), cutting lines (solid), and grain arrows. A few of the large patches have been "overlapped" by smaller ones. Where this is the case, the patch will be labeled for each of the patches. The larger patch includes all of the smaller patch and the extension, as well.

The sash and alternate block patches are too large to fit on the page; for these, half or quarter patterns are given, with dotted lines indicating the halfway fold. Do not place these on the fold of the fabric. Instead, place them on the fold of a large piece of paper, and use the completed paper pattern to cut the fabric.

The patterns are organized by shape, with each shape designated by a different letter. Within a shape, different sized patches are identified by different numbers. Patches are in alphabetical and numerical order so that you can find whichever ones you desire quickly and easily.

Most blocks call for patches to be cut with the grain indicated by the arrow. Occasionally, a pattern may be used in different blocks with the grain running different directions in each. In these cases, two grain arrows are given. Choose the grain arrow that puts the straight grain on the outside edges of the block.

Quilting motifs are given for the larger sash and alternate block patterns. These are presented with dashed lines well within the seam lines of the patch.

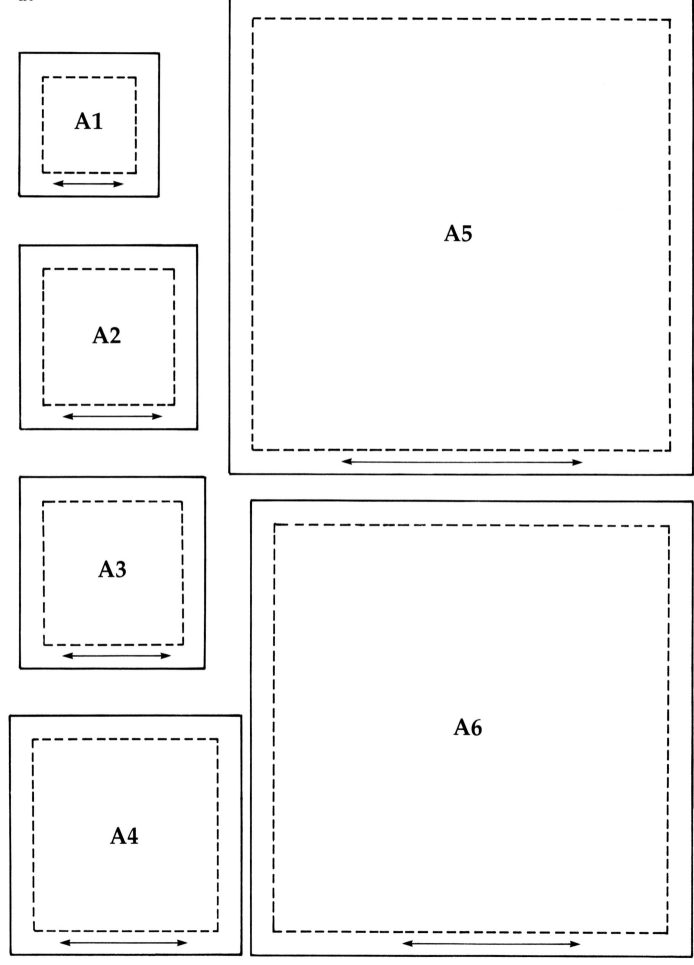

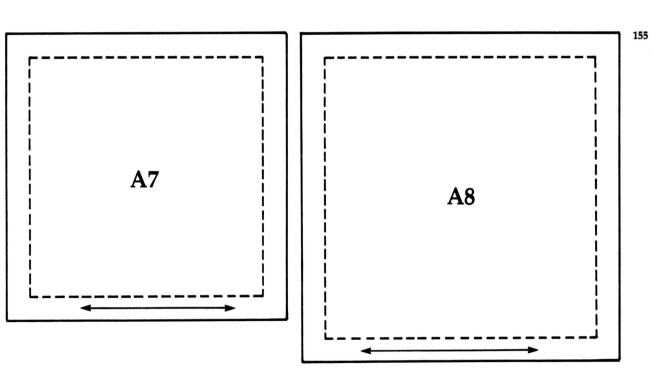

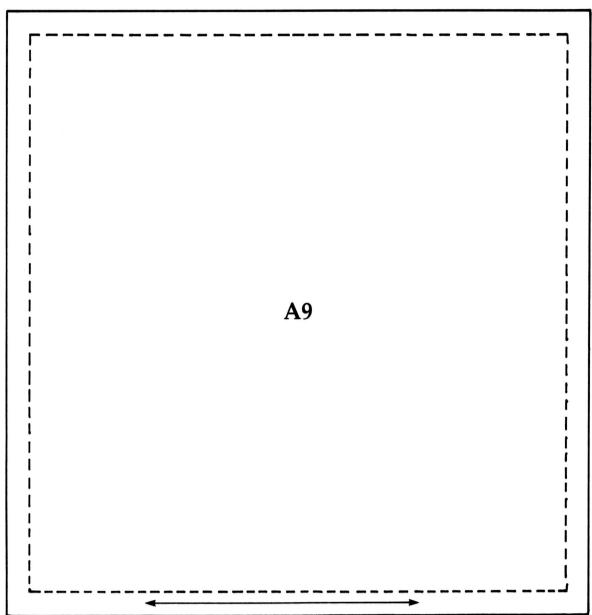

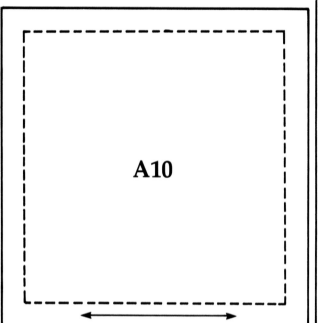

A10

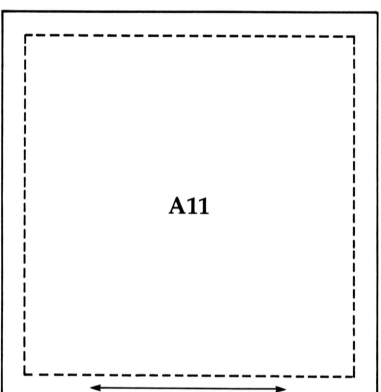

A11

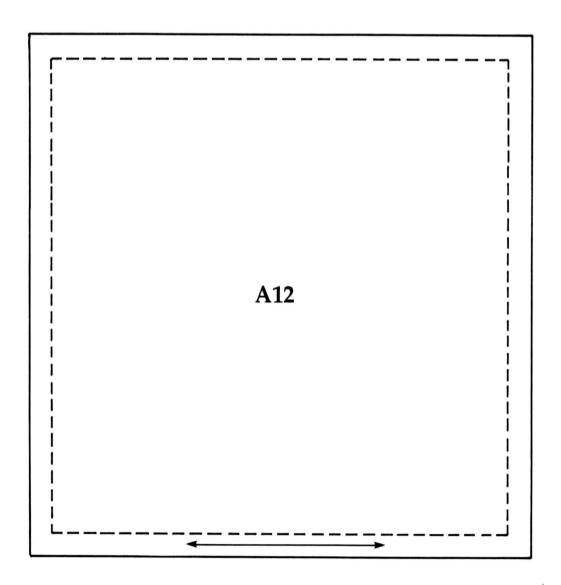

A12

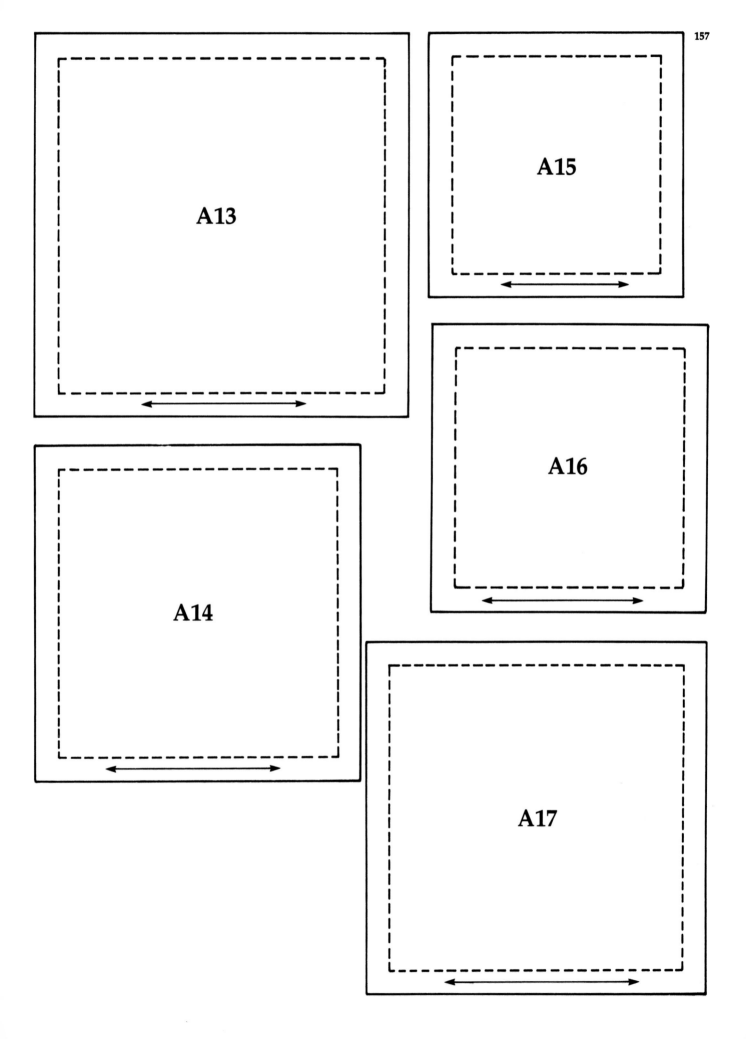

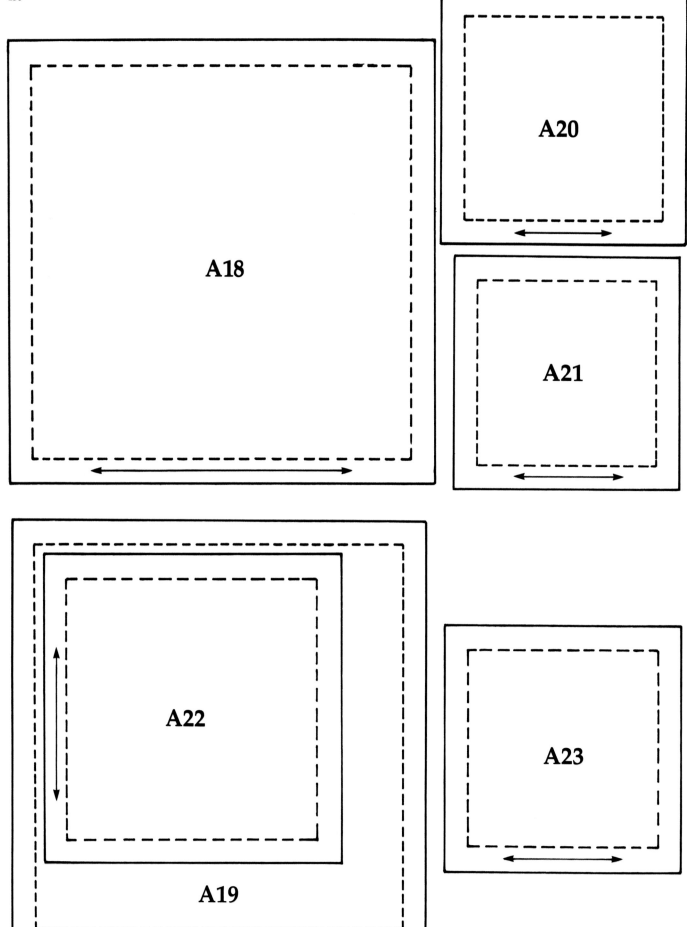

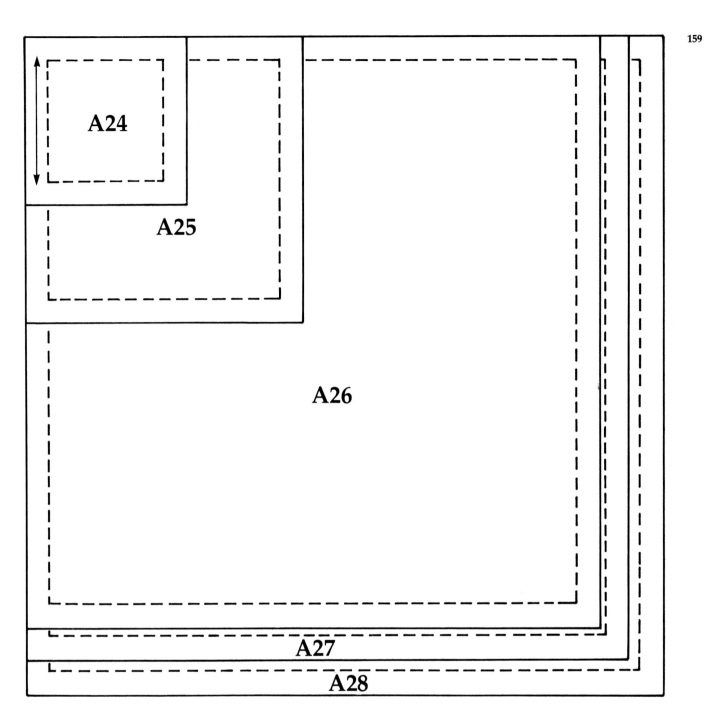

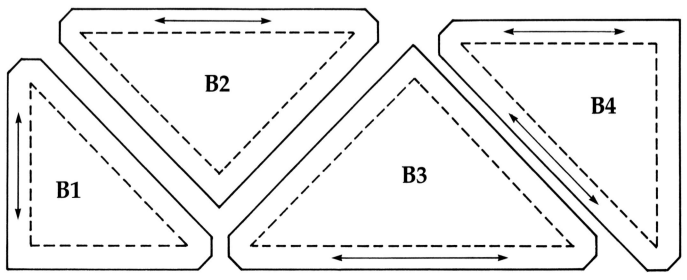

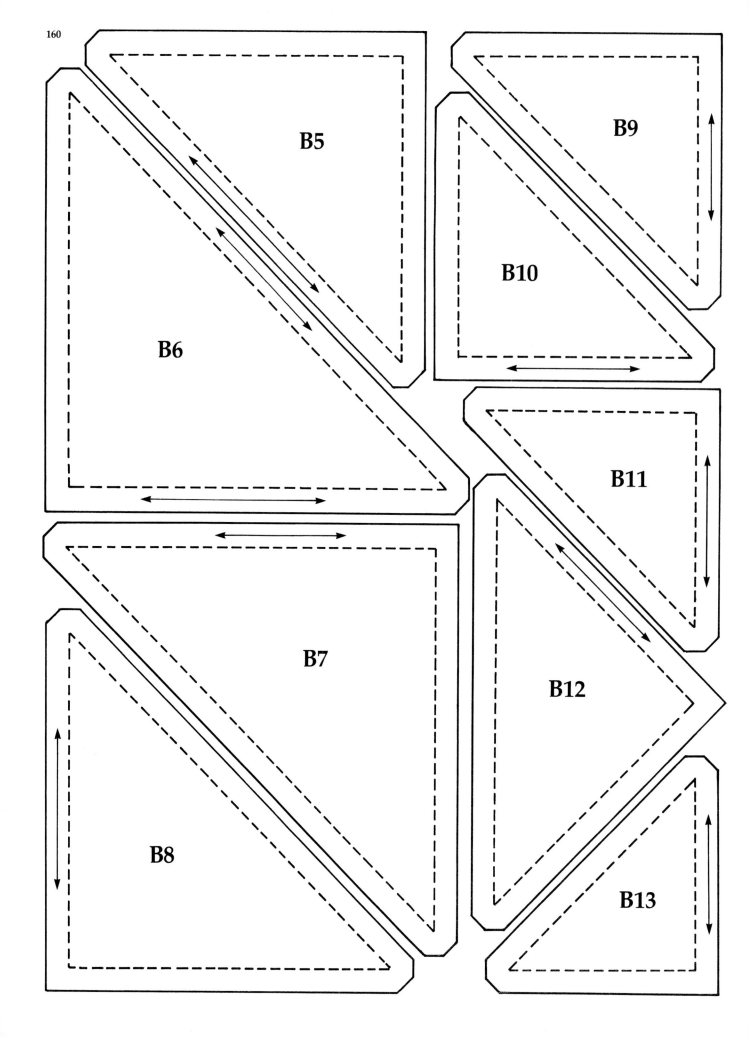

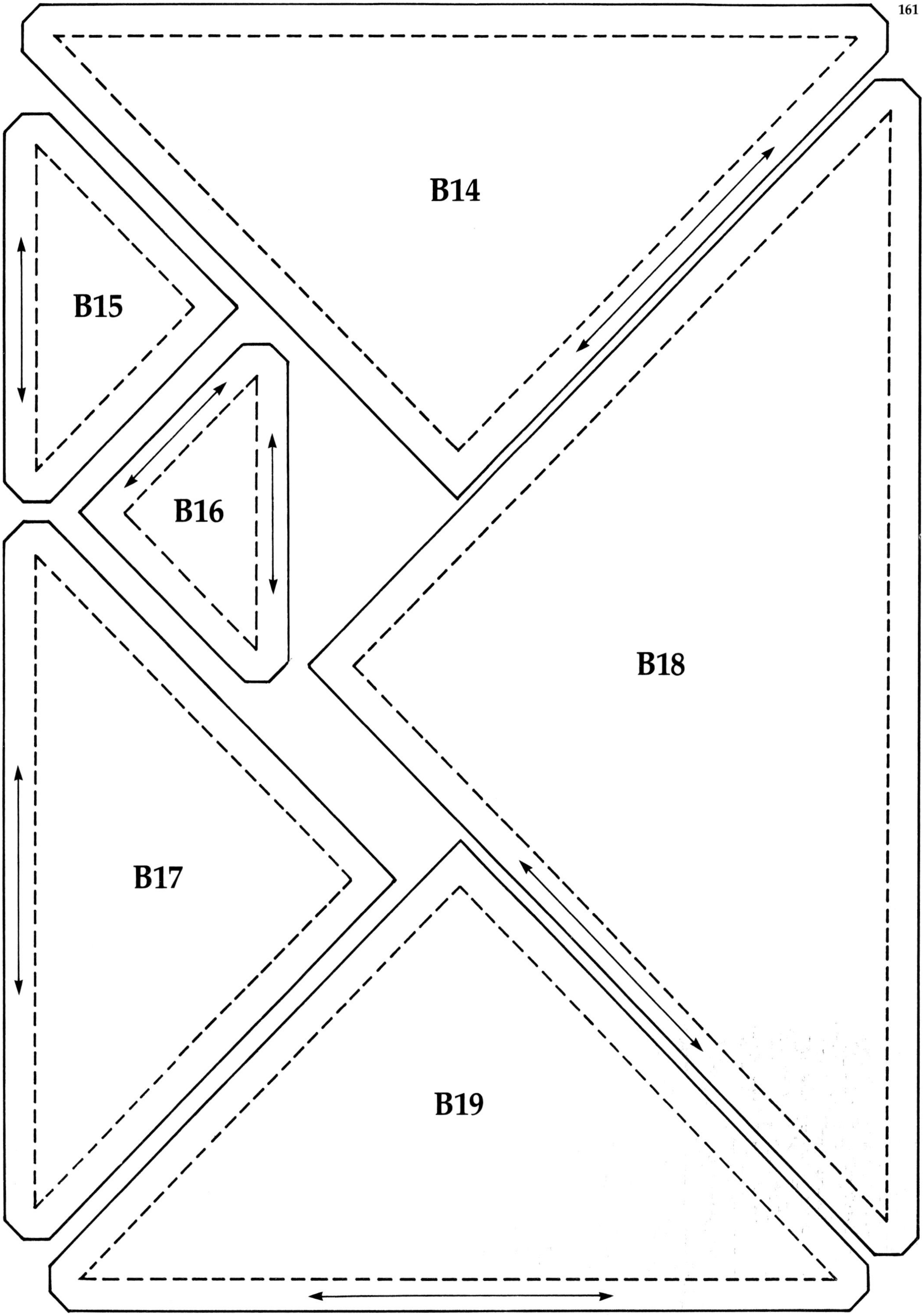

B14

B15

B16

B18

B17

B19

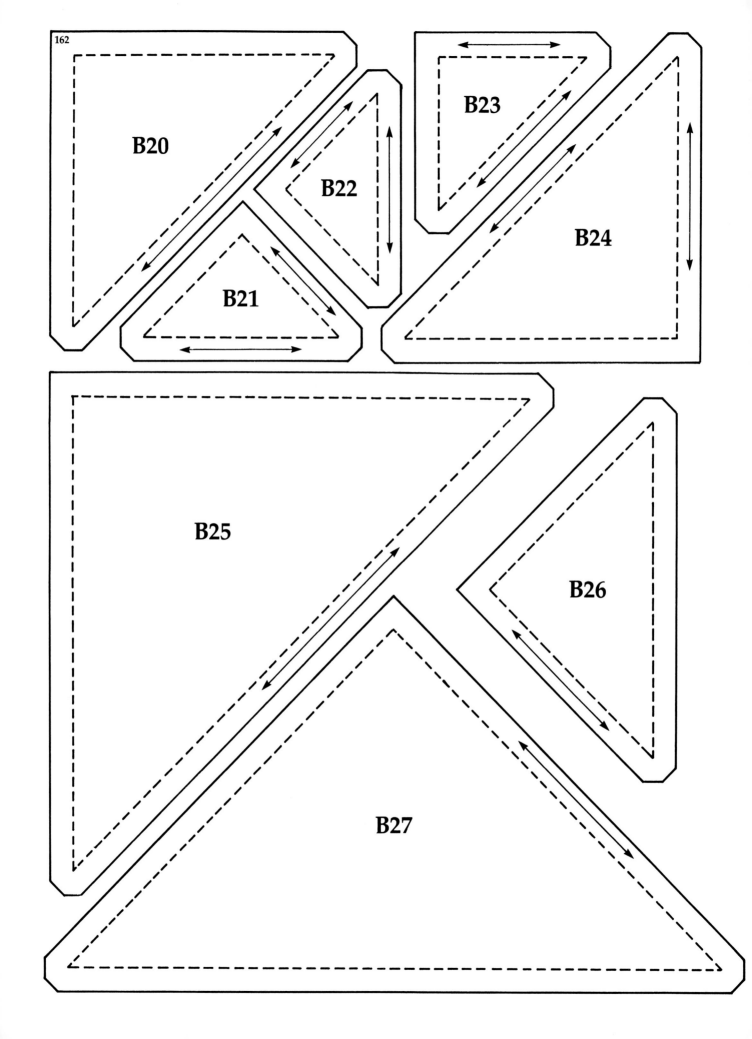

162

B20

B21

B22

B23

B24

B25

B26

B27

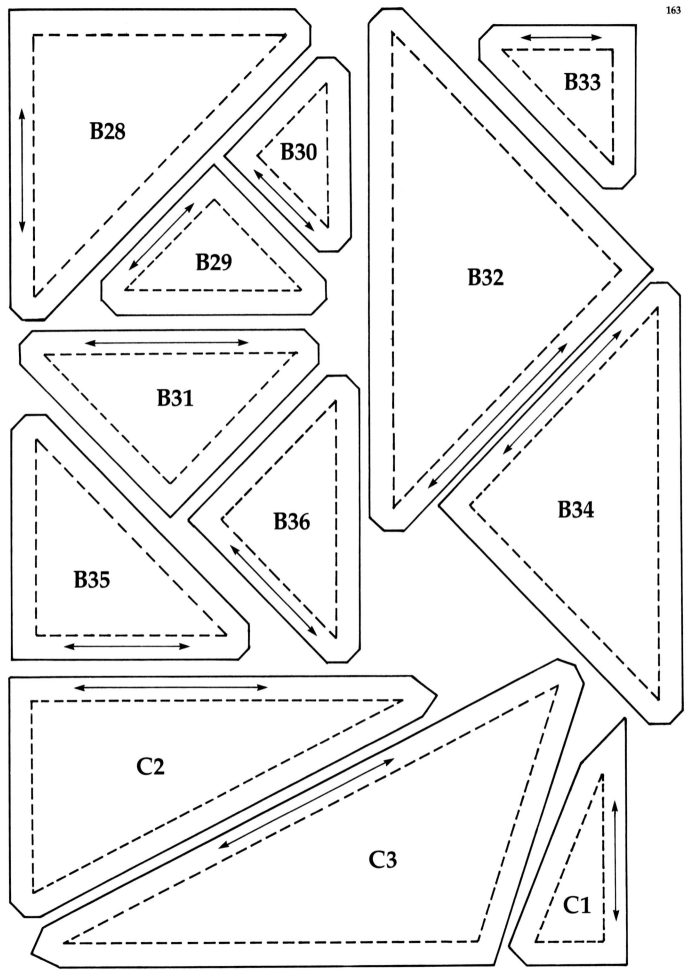

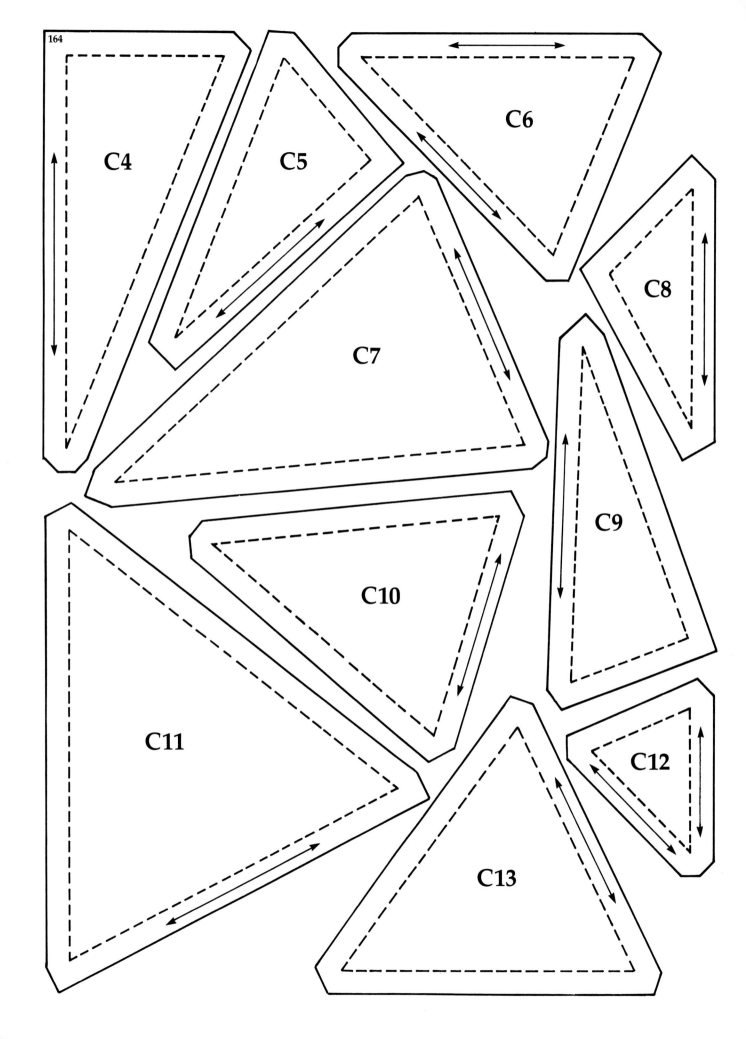

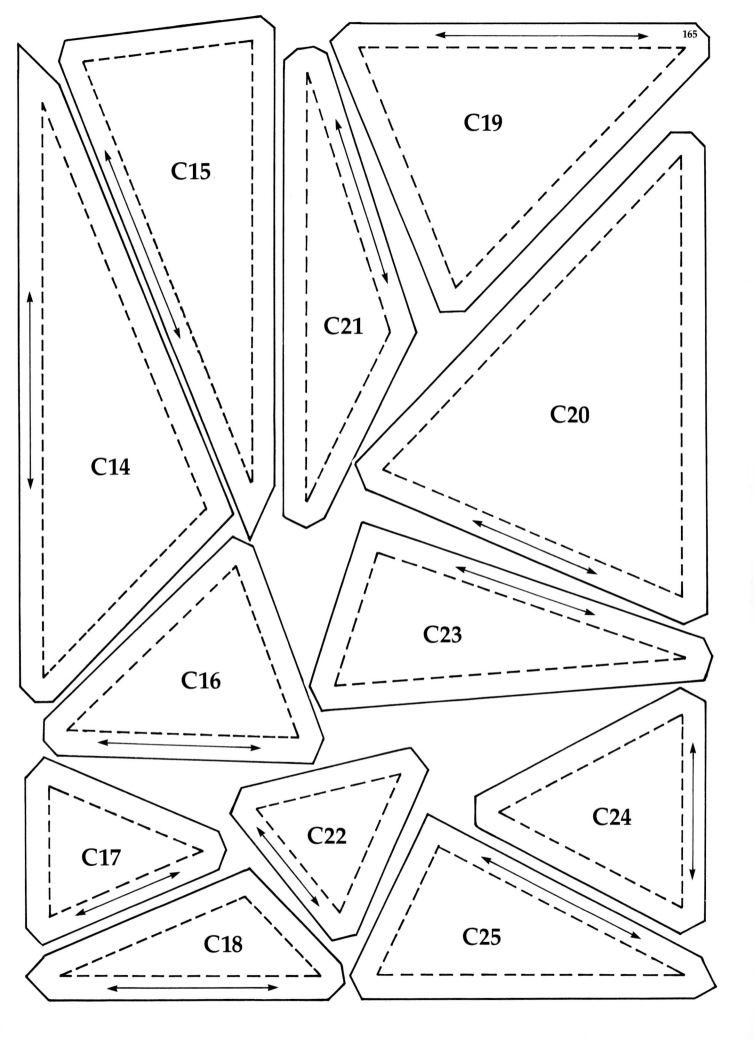

C15

C19

C14

C21

C20

C16

C23

C17

C22

C24

C18

C25

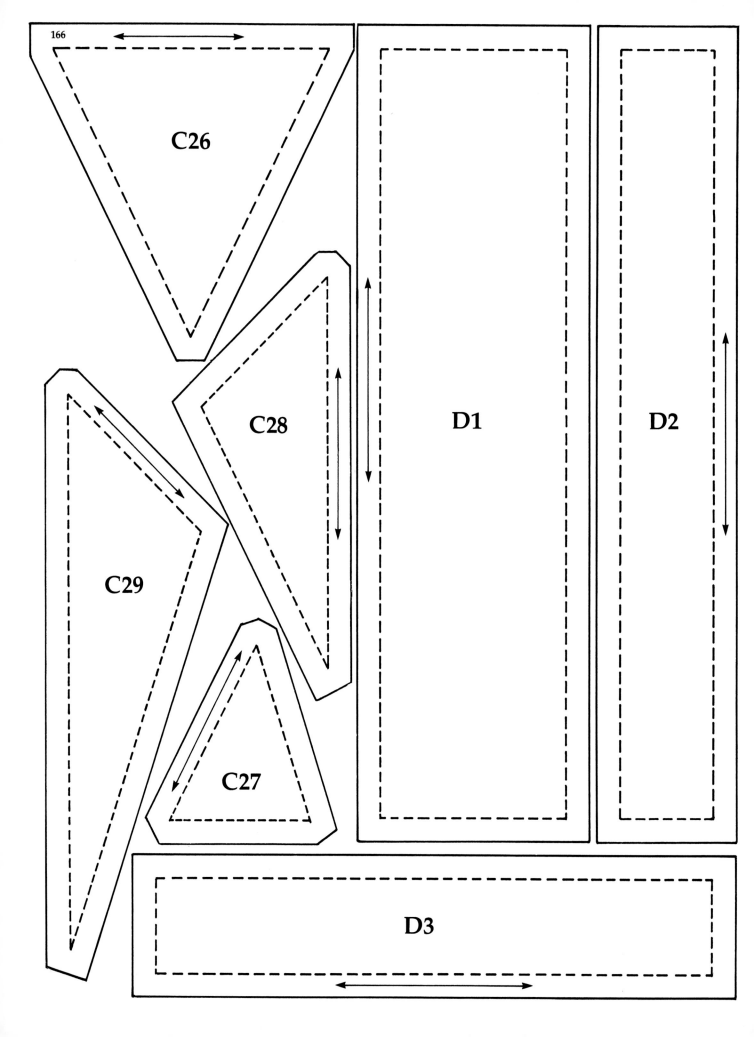

C26

C28

C29

C27

D1

D2

D3

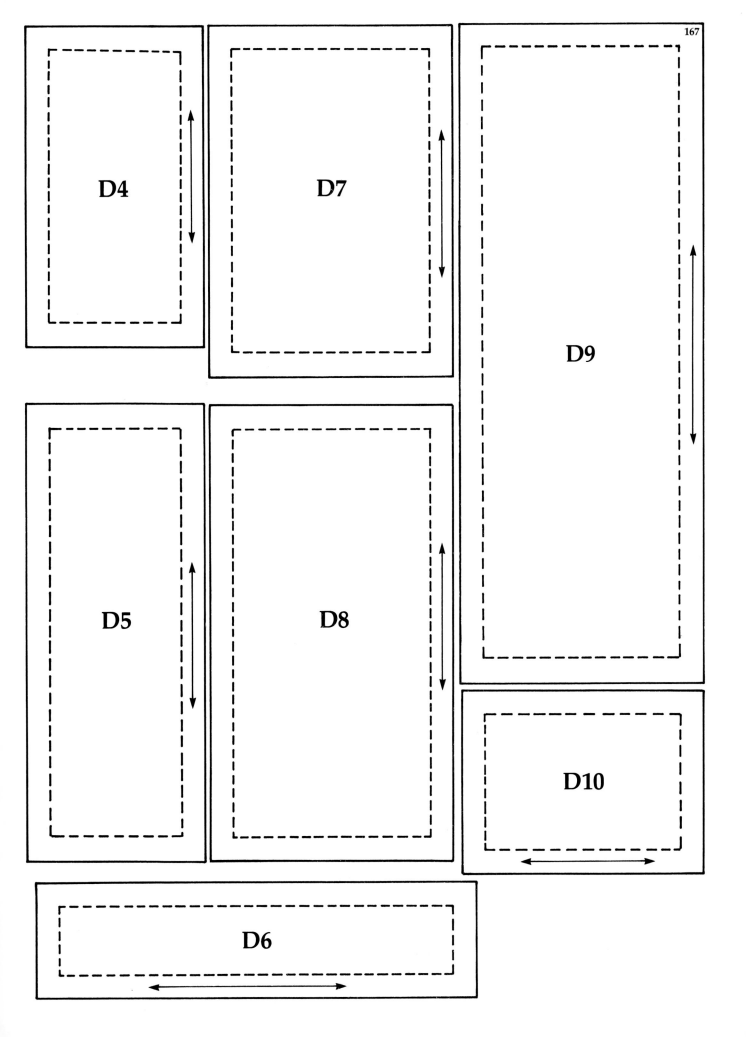

D11

D13

D15

D12

D14

D16

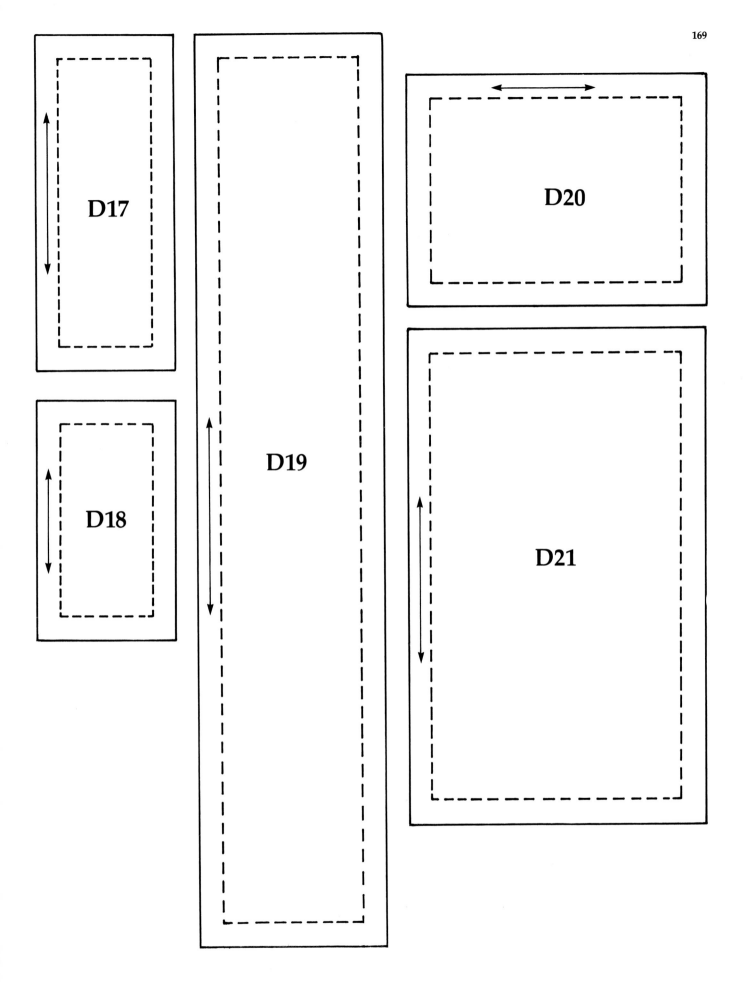

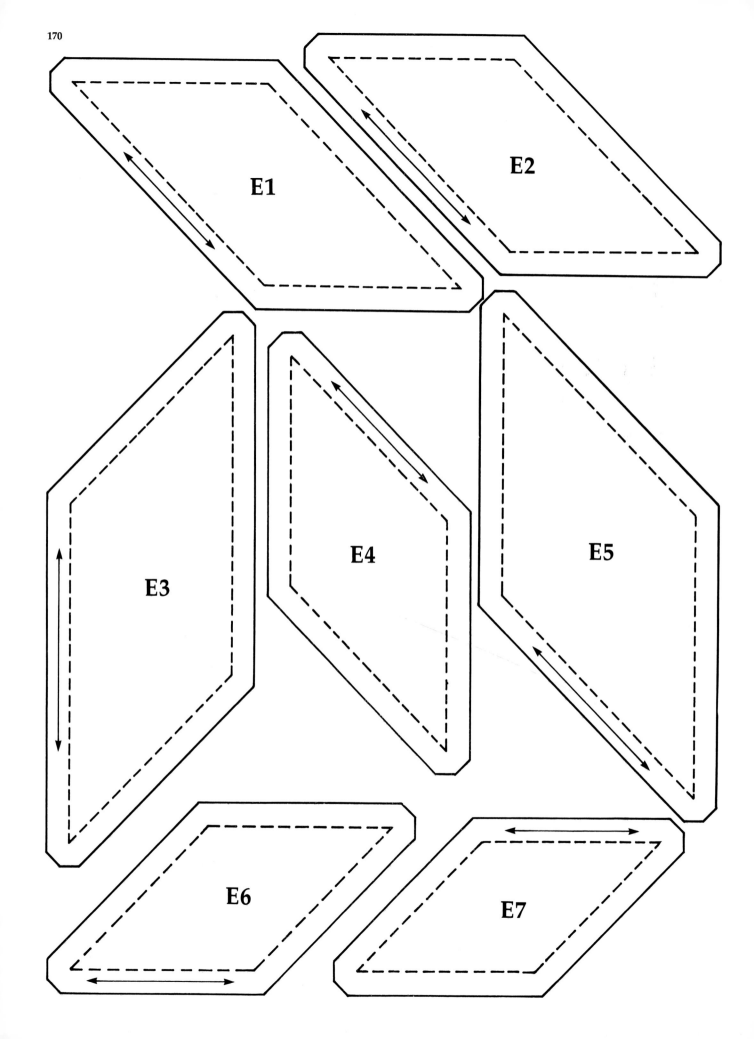

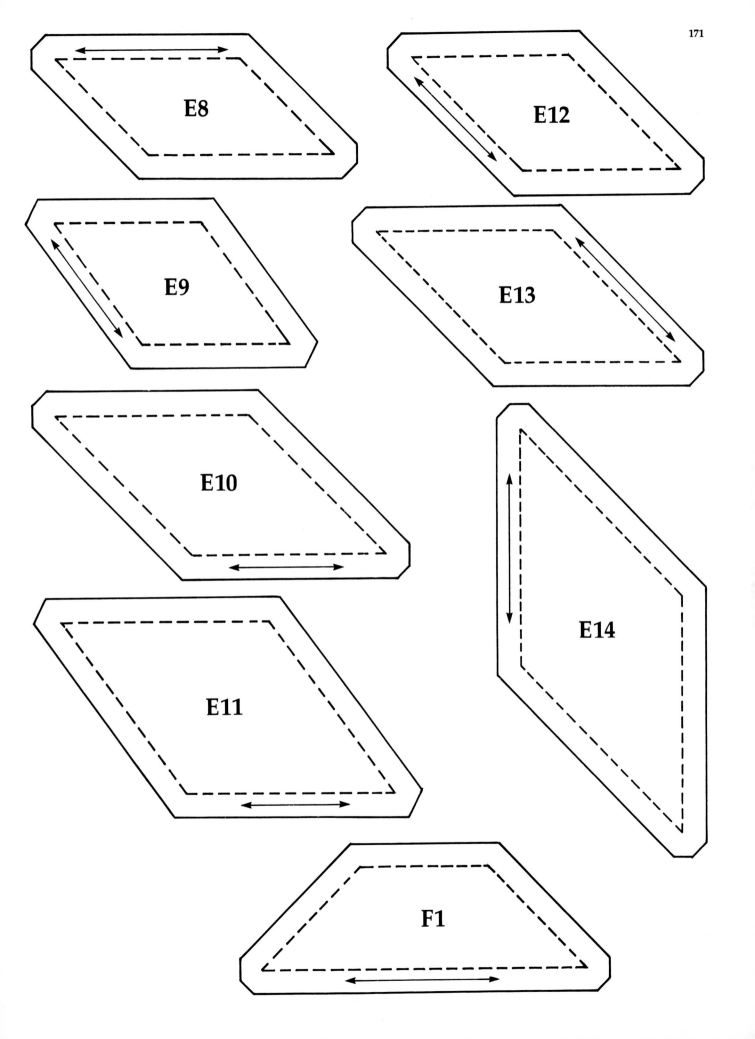

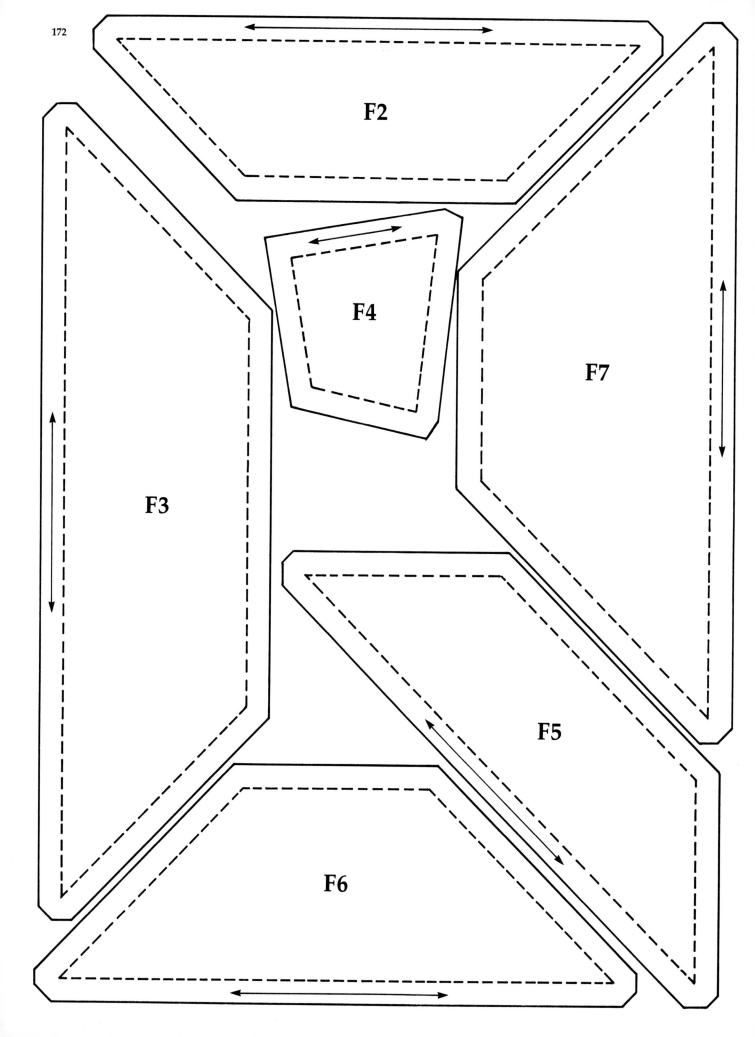

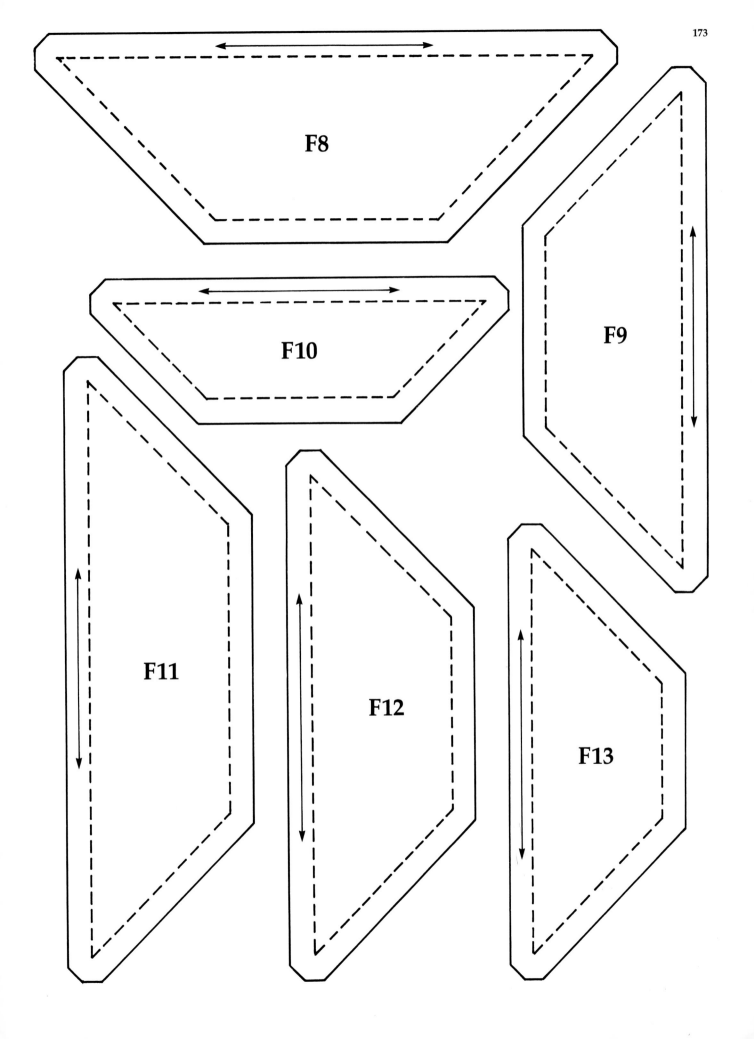

F8

F9

F10

F11

F12

F13

F14

F15

F16

F17

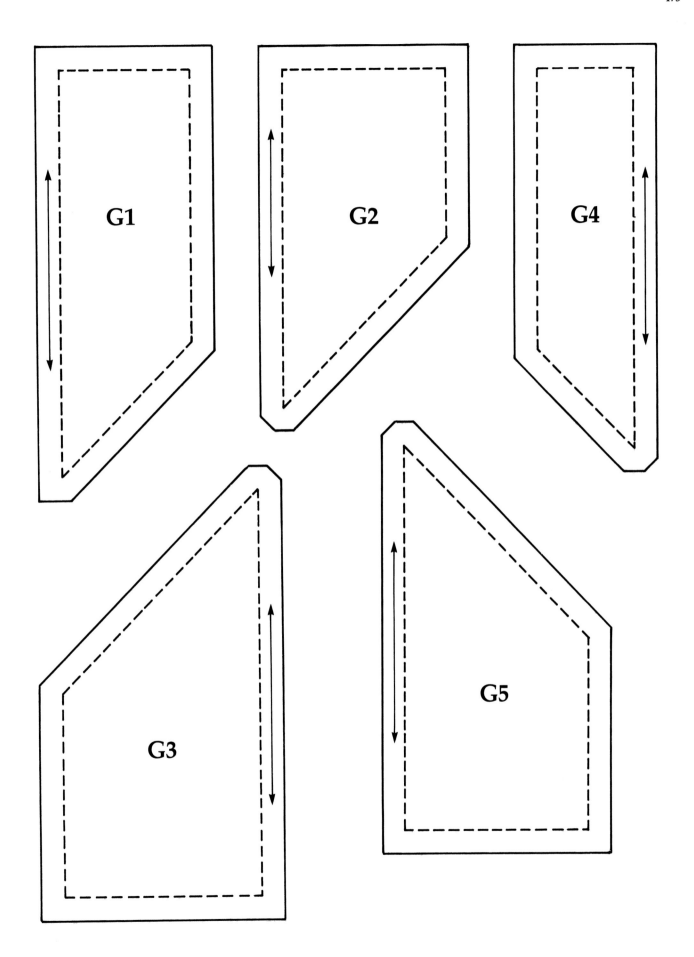

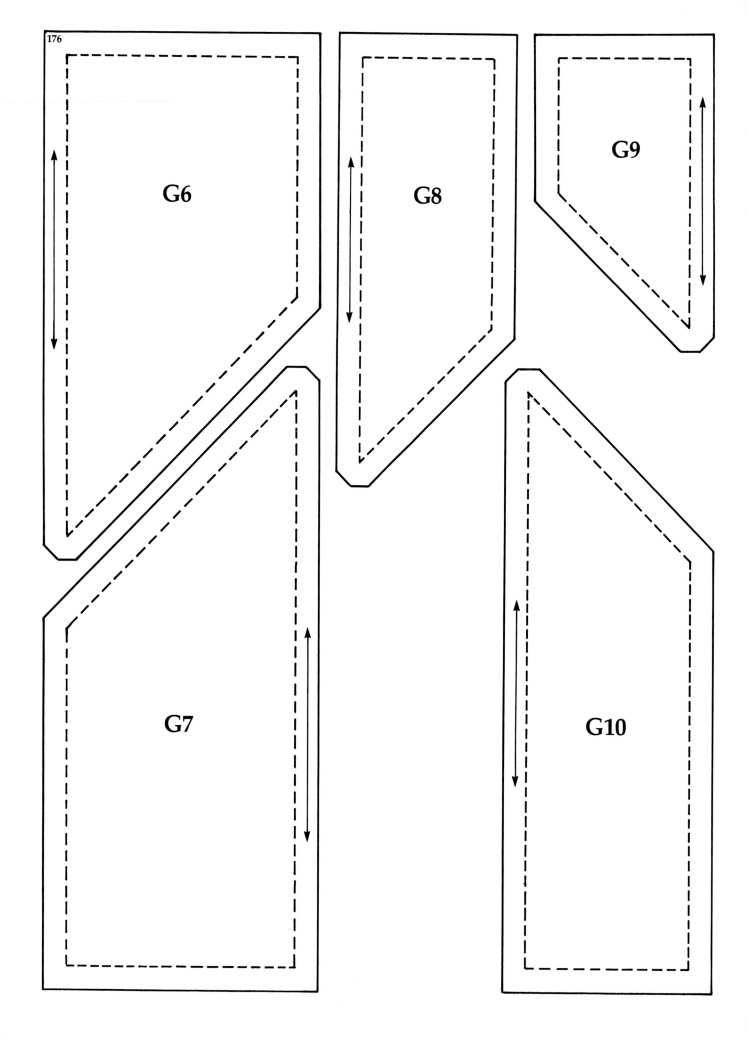

G6

G8

G9

G7

G10

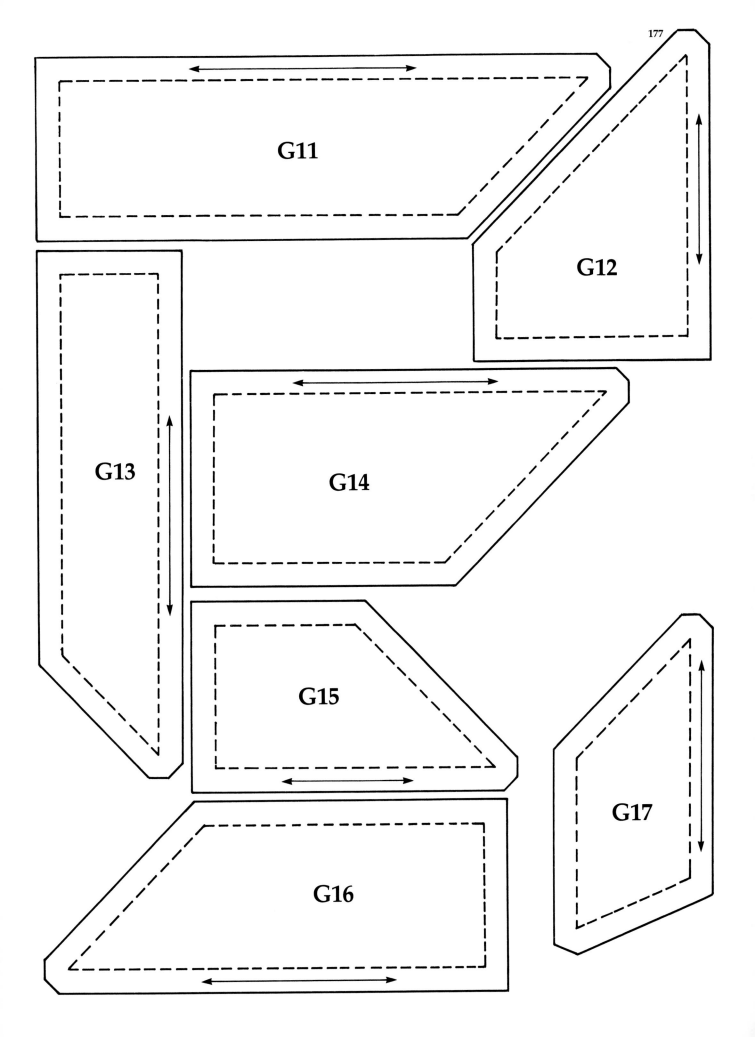

G11

G12

G13

G14

G15

G16

G17

G18

G19

G20

G21

G22

G23

H1

H2

H5

H3

H4

H6

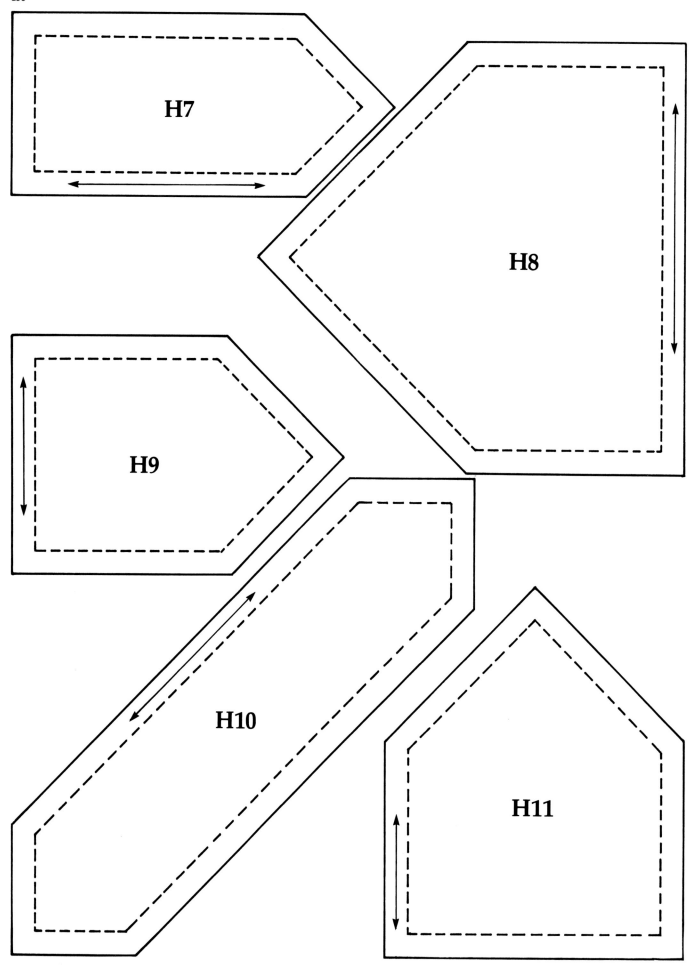

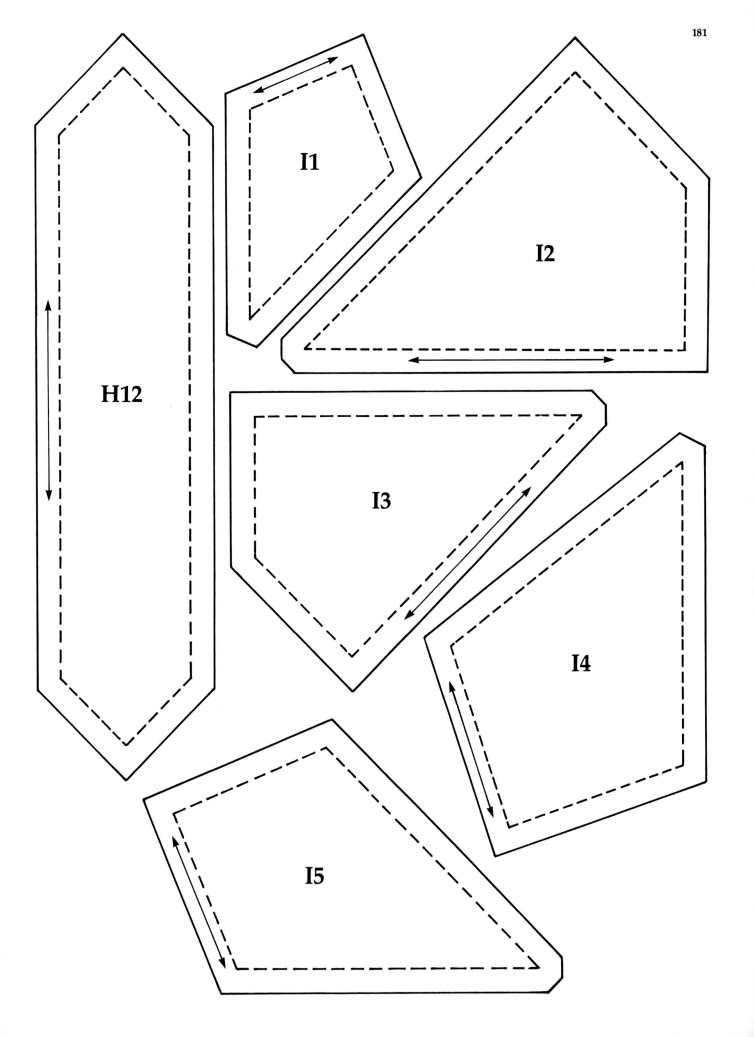

H12

I1

I2

I3

I4

I5

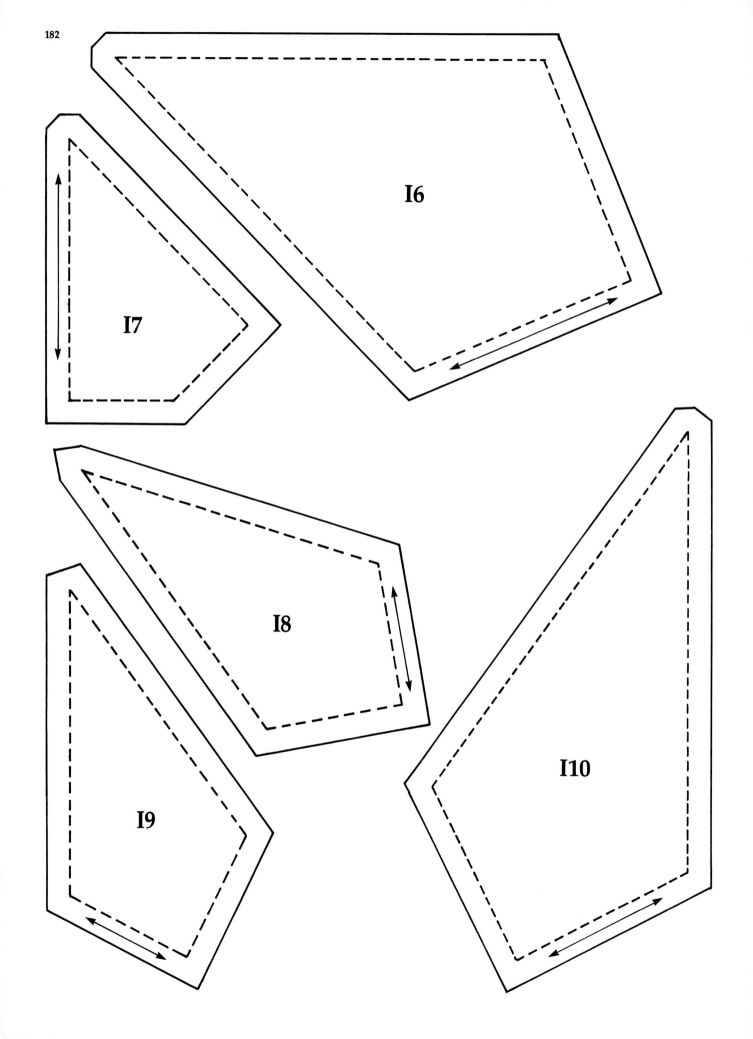

I6

I7

I8

I9

I10

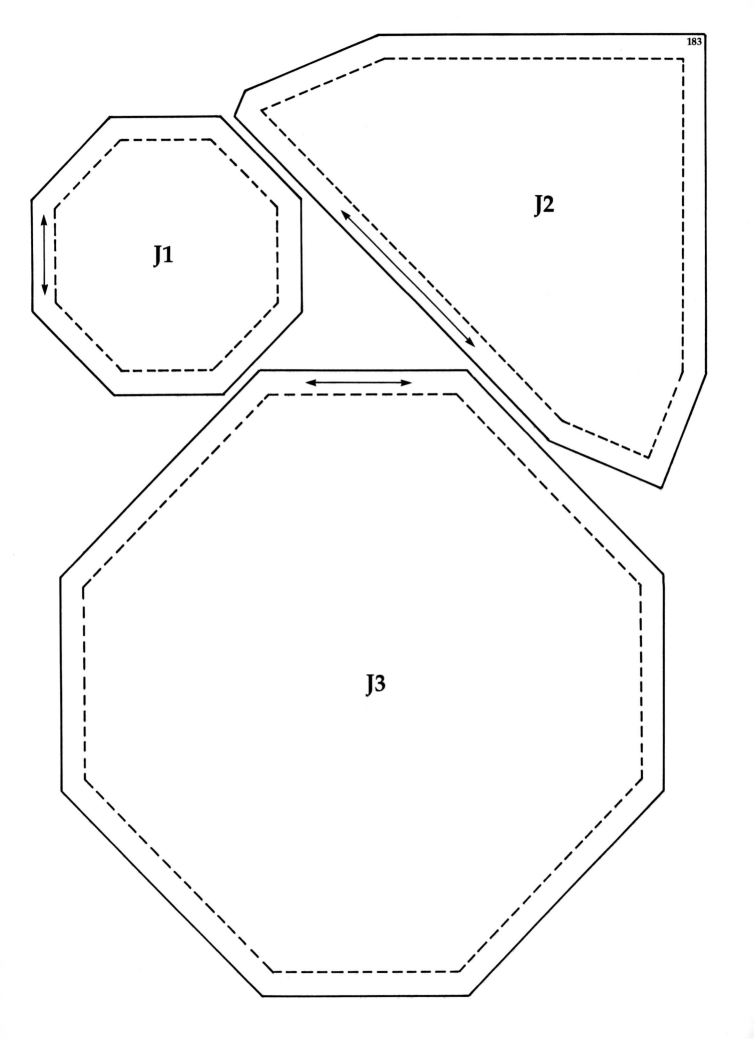

J1

J2

J3

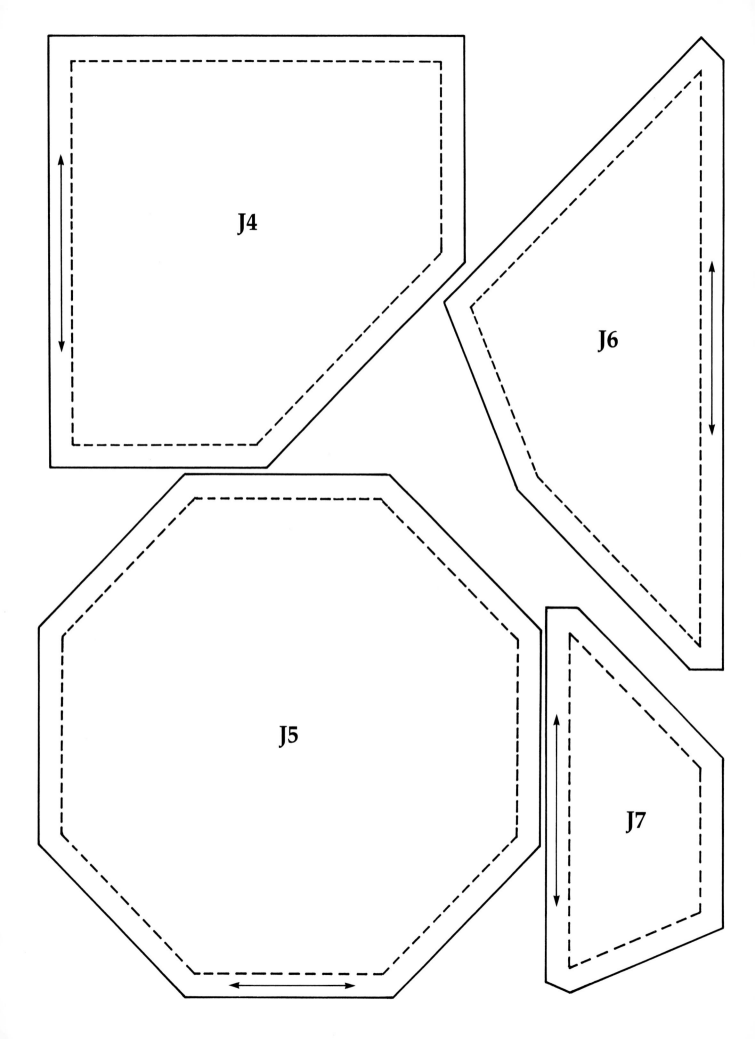

J4

J6

J5

J7

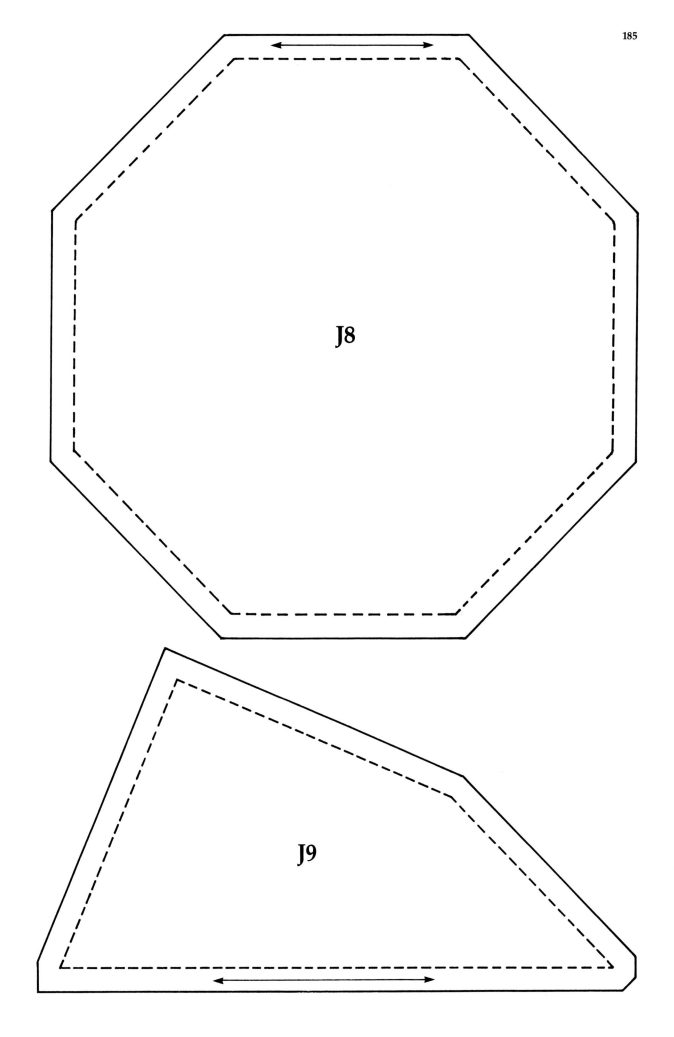

J8

J9

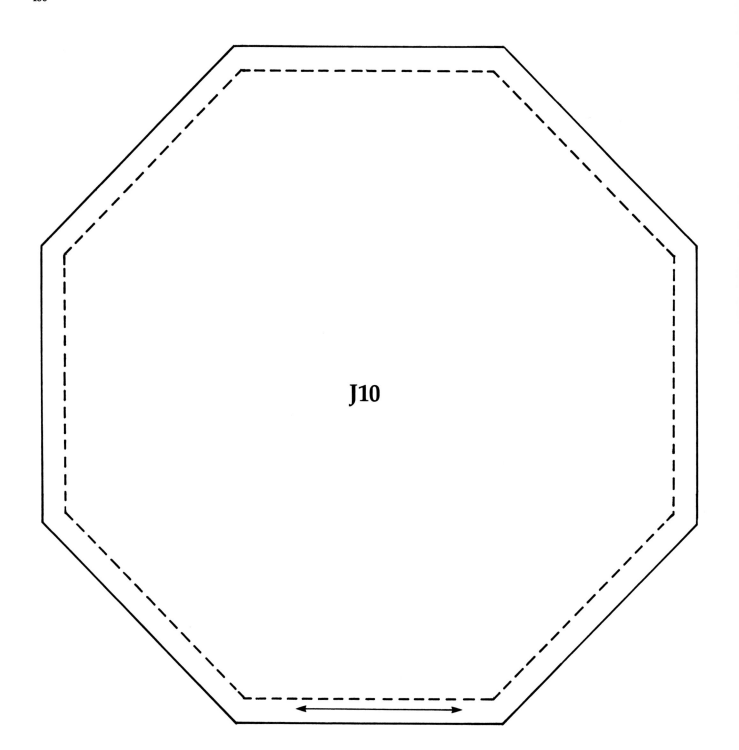

J10

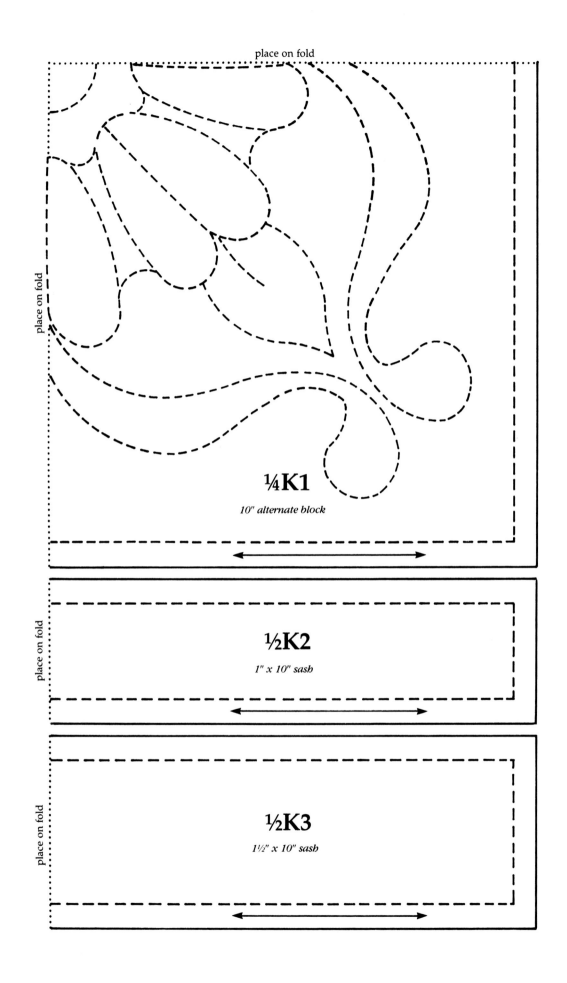

place on fold

place on fold

¼**K1**

10" alternate block

½**K2**

1" x 10" sash

place on fold

½**K3**

1½" x 10" sash

place on fold

188

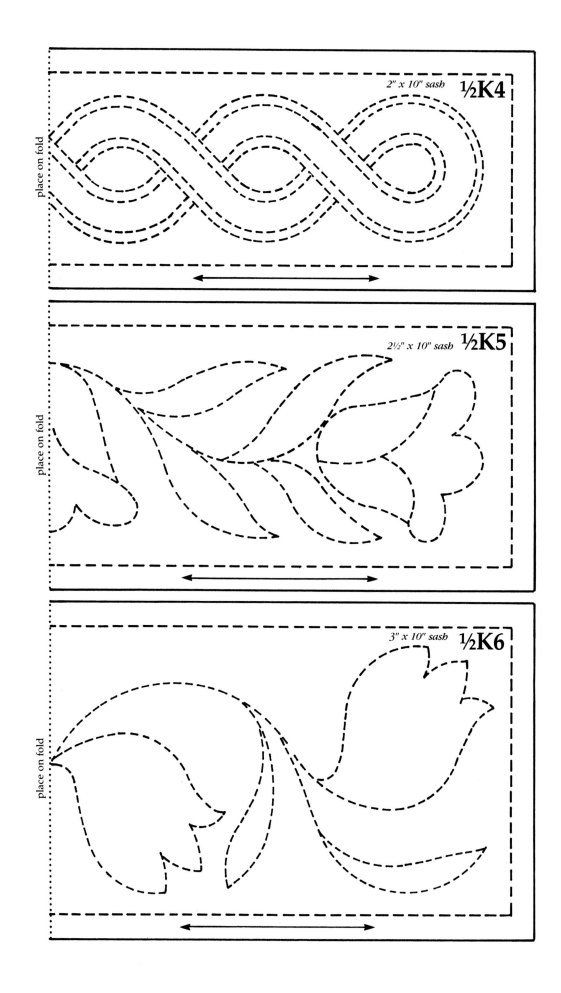

place on fold

2" x 10" sash   ½K4

place on fold

2½" x 10" sash   ½K5

place on fold

3" x 10" sash   ½K6

place on fold

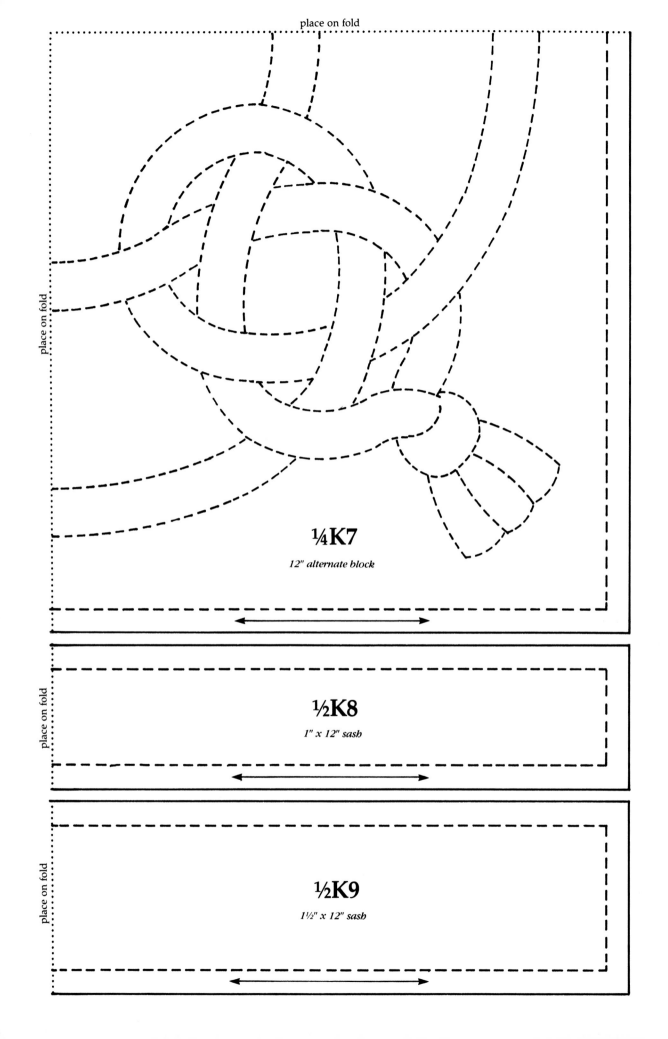

place on fold

¼K7

12" alternate block

place on fold

½K8

1" x 12" sash

place on fold

½K9

1½" x 12" sash

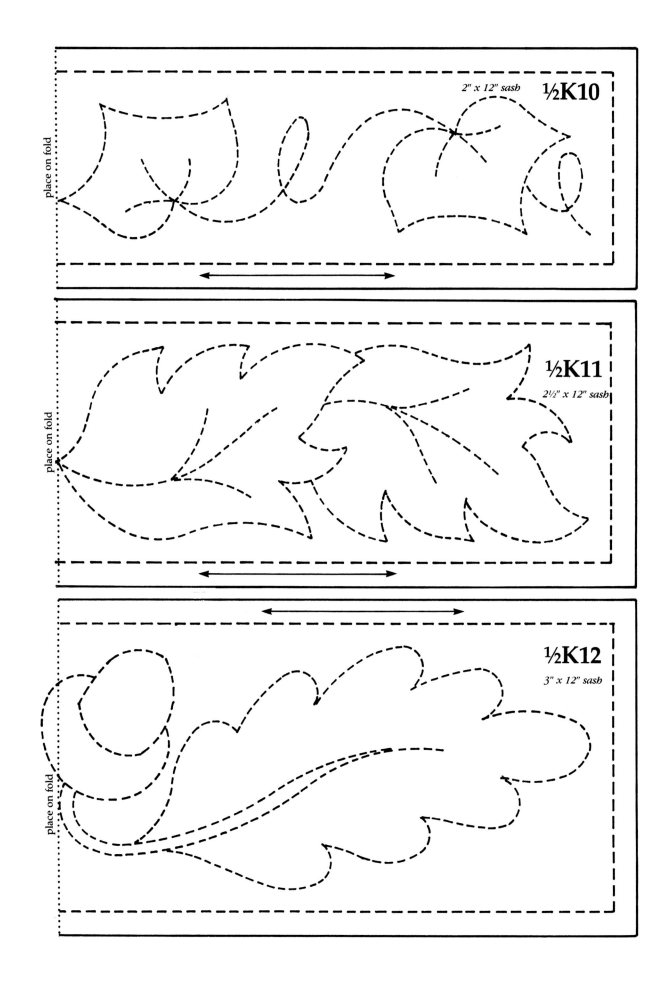

½K10

2" x 12" sash

place on fold

½K11

2½" x 12" sash

place on fold

½K12

3" x 12" sash

place on fold

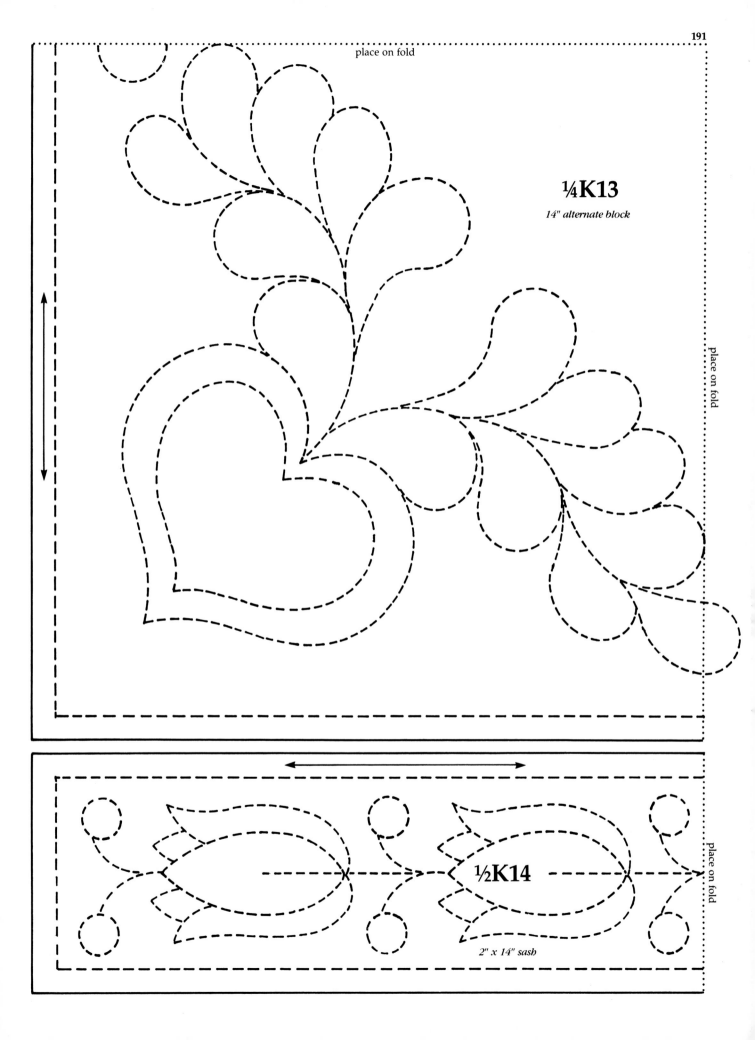

place on fold

place on fold

¼K13

14" alternate block

½K14

2" x 14" sash

place on fold

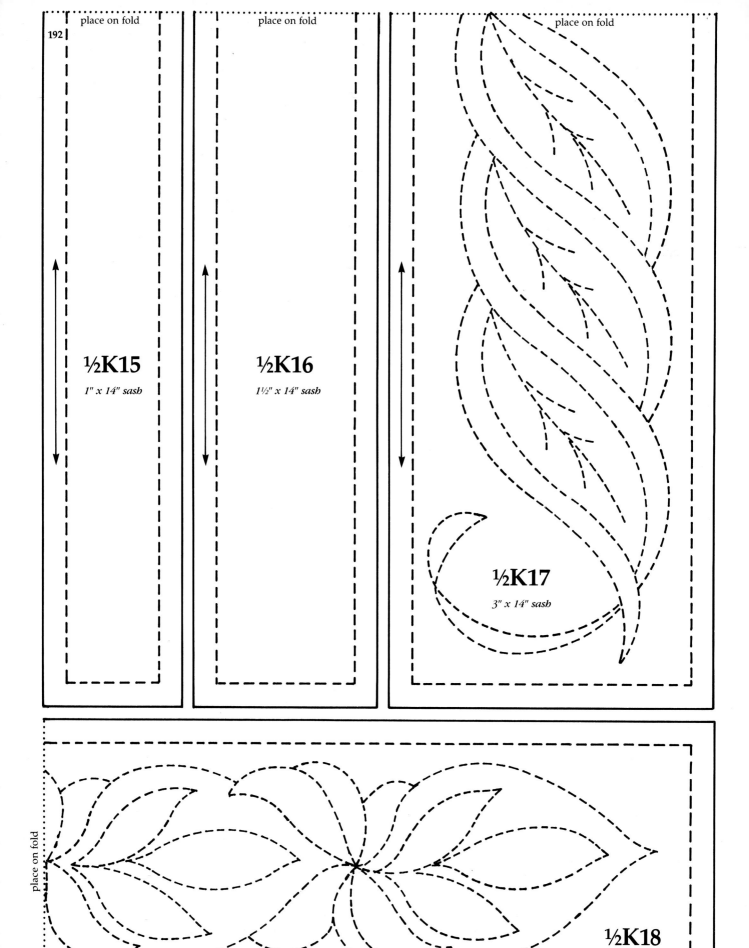

place on fold

place on fold

place on fold

½K15
1" x 14" sash

½K16
1½" x 14" sash

½K17
3" x 14" sash

place on fold

½K18
2½" x 14" sash